POTTED
HISTORIES

POTTED HISTORIES

HOW TO MAKE HOUSE PLANTS FEEL AT HOME

Paul Simons & John Ruthven

BBC Books

This book is published to accompany the
television series entitled *Potted Histories*
which was first broadcast in 1995

Published by BBC Books,
an imprint of BBC Worldwide Publishing Limited,
BBC Worldwide Ltd,
Woodlands, 80 Wood Lane
London W12 0TT

First published 1995
© Paul Simons and John Ruthven 1995
ISBN 0 563 37124 2

Designed by Tim Higgins
Photographs by Di Lewis
Set in Adobe Garamond
by Goodfellow and Egan Phototypesetting Ltd,
Cambridge
Printed in Great Britain by Cambus Litho Ltd,
East Kilbride
Bound in Great Britain by Hunter & Foulis Ltd,
Edinburgh
Colour separation by Dot Gradations Ltd,
near Chelmsford
Jacket printed by Lawrence Allen Ltd,
Weston-super-Mare

Contents

Acknowledgements

We would especially like to thank Paul Sturgess for his considerable horticultural advice and reading through the manuscript. Also thanks to Philip Goodson, University of Exeter, for reading through the cacti material.

Thanks also to:

Royal Botanic Gardens, Kew for making available their botanical knowledge, particularly David Cutler, Peter Brandham, Simon Mayo, Peter Boyce, David Simpson, Michael Simmons, Martin Sands, Hans Fliegner, Mike Maunder, Noel McGough; Madeleine Briggs, Flora and Fauna Preservation Society (FFPS); Andy Byfield, FFPS; Helen Kennedy, University of British Columbia, Canada; Sue Minter, Chelsea Physic Gardens; Inger Nordal, University of Oslo; Robert Crawford, University of St Andrews; Philip Grimes, University of Sheffield; Bill Wolverton, Plants for Clean Air; Adrian Whiteley, Royal Horticultural Society, Wisley; the librarians at the Lindley Library, Royal Horticultural Society; Tom Vogelmann, University of Wyoming; Bill Smith, University of Wyoming; Howard Griffiths, University of Newcastle; Anne Swithinbank; Wilhelm Barthlott, University of Bonn; Andrew Roth, Botanic Garden Company; David Lee, International University of Miami;

Chris Page, Royal Botanic Gardens, Edinburgh; Peter Wyse-Jackson, Botanic Gardens Conservation International; Peter James; Jim Ross, University of Reading; Martin Gibbons, Palm Centre, Putney; Mary Gibby, Natural History Museum; Sema Atay, Turkish society for nature conservation (DHKD); Arnoud Kwint and Miriam Akhtar.

Introduction

This is a very unusual house plant book – a cross between horticulture, natural history and botany. But why?

If you understand how house plants live in the wild, you're more likely to understand their needs in your home. That's what this book is all about. We've tried to translate the wild natural history of the plants into hardcore growing advice. It works very well for some plants, less well for others but wherever the relationship falls down we offer conventional horticultural information instead, so you're never left in the lurch.

This is a book aimed at the beginner who has been troubled by too much mumbo jumbo in other house plant books. And we've also catered for the experienced grower interested in the background stories of house plants – where they come from, how they're adapted to the wild, how this relates to their plant care, the history of their cultivation, and conservation.

House plants are foreign beings in your house and many of them are suffering a wretched life. They have personalities all of their own, and if only they could talk they would tell us to take more care of them.

The British are obsessed with their house plants; they've become 'green pets' to care for, dote over, and talk to. And they reward us by giving homes, offices, and hospitals a more relaxing atmosphere. New research shows that indoor plants even have amazing powers of cleansing: they help get rid of dust, pollution and bad smells from the air.

Yet we seem to be bamboozled by house plants. Why do rubber plants turn brown and drop their leaves, cyclamens refuse to flower and Venus flytraps rot? Even tough things such as spider plants sometimes go horribly sick.

If you want to understand your house plants you need to appreciate how their ancestors lived in the wild. For instance, if you know that cyclamens come from

Mediterranean climates, it's easier to appreciate why they need cool damp conditions to flower in early spring, and rest during the summer heat and drought. Unfortunately we tend to keep them too warm and then they shrivel up because they think it's summer.

This book is the first ever guide to the natural history of house plants, based on the television series *Potted Histories*, made by BBC Television's Natural History Unit. For the book, we have chosen 108 plants, mostly common species, but we have also included a few exotic ones such as the carnivorous plants. Each plant has its own 'biography' – a sort of curriculum vitae to show where it originally came from, what life in its wild home was like and why it behaves the way it does in the home. It also includes first-aid advice for the ailing pot plant, based on what we know of its home background.

A Survival Guide to House Plants

It is hardly surprising that house plants often have a hard time. Their original ancestors came from far off exotic places – deserts, tropical rainforests, mountains, for example – so why should they feel at home on top of the television set in cold draughts, dry air, cold nights, and having coffee slops poured over them? No wonder they're so often under stress.

Woe betide if you use your house plants simply as bits of interior decor. The real art of growing house plants is to understand their origins and match each plant to the right conditions in your home, not to cross your fingers and hope that a fantastic exotic will survive just because you want it to. We've got to start thinking of the best room or part of a room for a plant to be at home in.

Also, because you are very much part of the life-support system of your house plants you must know their needs – water, minerals, light and air.

Water is vital for the plant's chemistry, keeping it upright, and carrying food inside the plant. But too much or too little water can easily kill a house plant, so knowing the water and drainage conditions in the wild is often helpful.

Minerals are needed for growth and development, but some minerals are needed in large amounts – nitrogen, potassium and phosphates – while many others are needed in trace amounts, such as iron, boron, magnesium. But different plants have evolved to cope with different soils, so knowing the original soil of their ancestors is often helpful.

Light is vital for photosynthesis – the miracle of plantlife which turns water and carbon dioxide into sugars. Light also keeps plants in tune with the world around them. So knowing why different plants need different light conditions is crucial for understanding where to place them in the house. Bear in mind that those conditions change during the day and during the year – strong summer daylight fades into weak winter light, and this has an enormous effect on house plants.

Versatility

But having said how important it is to understand their needs, plants are also versatile organisms. Despite what many indoor gardening books tell you, house plants can often adjust to a rough life in your home. They can reorganize their photosynthesis to compensate for shade, or slowly adapt to cooler temperatures, dry air or lack of water. And even when they suffer from neglect, there are other compensations, such as having no animals to eat them, no other plants to fight off, and plenty of rich carbon dioxide to 'breathe' in.

So that is why growing house plants by trial and error sometimes works. It's also why much of the information we've given for each plant is approximate. For instance, the temperature ranges for growing each plant are only a guide, and that's why we've also used loose descriptions such as 'cool' and 'warm'. If you're not sure about the temperature ranges in your rooms it's worth taking measurements with an ordinary thermometer or buying a minimum/maximum thermometer which shows the coolest and warmest temperature. If you don't want to go to the expense of buying a thermometer, a central heating thermostat gives an idea of what the warmest temperature in a room is.

Common mistakes and how to avoid them

Even though house plants come from all over the world, there are still a few basic tips on looking after most of them.

They usually hate sudden shocks, such as knocks, blasts of cold air, violent shaking and being uprooted. This is particularly true of plants from fairly stable environments, for example tropical forest floors where conditions stay fairly constant most of the time.

Very often plants get upset by a quick change in temperature rather than the actual temperature itself, whether low or high. So slow temperature changes put the plant under far less stress. It is amazing to see tropical plants being sold outside in markets in the freezing cold – if you do buy a tropical plant in a very cold atmosphere it may be suffering intolerable stress and may be already dying. Another shock you can give a house plant is a dose of cold water straight from the tap – it's like giving it a cold shower on its most sensitive parts! The tips of roots are especially sensitive to temperature, and warmth-loving plants such as African violets can easily be hurt by cold water. Simply leave water to stand at room temperature before supplying the plant.

Knowing how much watering a plant needs is also a tricky business. Gardening books have a habit of talking in unspecific terms like 'well watered', 'good soaking', 'water sparingly' – which are of little help to the beginner. One of the commonest errors is to keep a plant standing in water. See it from the plant's point of view. It grows in a small pot and if it is steeped in water the soil rapidly becomes

waterlogged. About 65 per cent of soil is made up of air-filled spaces between particles of earth, and these provide essential oxygen for the roots to 'breathe'. If those air spaces become clogged with water the roots become starved of oxygen, and often rot. And if the roots don't die from rot they get poisoned by a sudden rush of toxins when the soil dries out again.

A lot of the watering problems can be solved by giving the plant the right mixture of soil and gravel. The aim is to make an airy soil that helps prevent waterlogging, but at the same time is thick enough to hold sufficient water. The pot should have a little coarse gravel or bits of broken terracotta in the bottom for drainage. A good rule of thumb is to cover the gravel with an equal mixture of soil-based compost such as John Innes No 2, and soilless peat or so-called coir compost. Coir, by the way, is a peat-free compost made from coconut husks and is now used as an alternative to peat, to avoid the commercial digging of peat from valuable boglands which need to be conserved (and where, incidentally, many of our carnivorous plants grow).

Of course, underwatering is just as big a hazard, because there comes a point when a plant wilts and can't recover. So make sure a plant's soil never turns completely bone dry. For most plants wait until the top of the soil turns dry and then soak it until water just starts to drip from the bottom of its pot.

There is also a seasonal aspect to watering. Plants such as cacti and other dryland plants, which go into 'hibernation' and stop growing in winter, need to be kept dry overwinter otherwise they're liable to rot or grow thin and gangly and fail to flower the following summer.

Apart from water for their roots, most house plants crave moisture from the air. Plants lose water from their leaves and even if their soil is well watered most species enjoy humidity. The big problem is that our homes are so warm and dry they feel like deserts to the average plant and for humidity-loving species dry air often turns their leaves yellow and brittle. The easiest solution is to raise humidity around the plant with a choice of devices:

- ○ standing them on a tray of wet sand or pebbles
- ○ standing a pot plant in a pot filled with wet peat
- ○ standing plants next to open saucers of water
- ○ standing groups of them together to share each other's moisture
- ○ misting plants daily, preferably in early morning, using a mister to make very fine droplets of water and only sufficient to put a thin film of droplets on the plant helps

But a word of warning about misting plants with water or pouring water over their leaves. A lot of plants don't enjoy heavy watering on their leaves because it chokes their 'breathing' pores and sometimes sets off infection. This is especially true of African violets which easily rot if water gets into their leaf rosettes. In fact they are so delicate that large drops of water on their leaves act like a magnifying glass under the sun and scorches the leaves.

Too much or too little light can be a problem, depending on where the plant originally comes from. A plant from shady places, such as tropical forest floors, doesn't enjoy a bright, hot sunny windowsill. On the other hand, there are very few plants that can cope with living in darkness. The compromise is to stand shade plants away from too much direct sunlight in summer – but in winter the sun is so weak they can probably take a bright windowsill. For plants from bright environments, such as deserts, winter time can be a problem, and many of them, for example cacti, go into 'hibernation' when they need to be kept cool and dry.

Light is a real bugbear in winter because the day length is so short and the quality of light so insipid. Plants can be moved closer to windowsills – assuming it is sunny – or a more

dramatic top-up can be used with artificial light. Unfortunately the ordinary artificial light in our homes is no good for plant growth because it's too weak and the wrong colour. Plants are very fussy about their light and need the blues and reds from daylight. Now our ordinary domestic light bulbs are very poor in these colours, and are very weak in energy. So we need to mimic ordinary daylight, using either fluorescent lights or special 'grow lamps' you can buy at electrical shops. But unless the lights are extremely powerful, they usually need to be about 30 – 60cm (1 – 2ft) away from the plant – simply using fluorescent lights on the ceiling doesn't work!

Myths and legends

FEEDING PLANTS CIGARETTE ASH AND BEER

Cigarette ash is rich in phosphates, one of the essential minerals plants need in large amounts. But tobacco itself is actually a poison which can harm many plants, so tipping out ash-trays into plant pots is not a good idea.

Tipping out unwanted drinks into pots is liable to give plants quite a hangover, because beer and any other alcohol can damage plant roots by making them lose water and minerals. And it's no good offering a reviving cup of cold coffee or tea because in large enough volumes they'll poison roots too.

TALKING TO PLANTS

Talking to plants is quite good for them. Plants need carbon dioxide for photosynthesis, but most of the time they're starved of it because there is only a trifling 300 parts per million of the gas in the air. Yet every time we talk to plants we give them a short and intense burst of about 50,000 parts per million which enriches them. Even having people or pets in a room will raise the level of carbon dioxide and do the plants good. Also, talking to plants blows off dust choking their leaf pores, helping them 'breathe' more easily.

PLAYING MUSIC TO PLANTS

This is a little bit of a controversial subject because so much of the research on it is unverified, but wouldn't it be nice if it was true? So take heart, because there is some evidence that playing certain types of music, for example male choirs and female solo voices, can stimulate growth. The explanation is probably that certain sound frequencies vibrate the plant, perhaps helping it carry its food.

STROKING PLANTS

Touching plants has some surprising effects. Daily stroking of a plant stem will make its stem shorter and wider, which in the wild is a useful way to stand up to the wind. But for reasons we still don't understand, stroking also boosts a plant's tolerance to drought, cold and even insect attack. Japanese farmers have long used this phenomenon by stroking sugar beet seedlings before transplanting them to the field to help them survive and flourish. Recent research also reveals that stroking plants helps them fight off aphids, for reasons no one can fathom out yet.

USING AN ASPIRIN IN A VASE
OF CUT FLOWERS

It may seem strange to think that aspirin could have any effect on plants, but aspirin was actually made from plants until the turn of this century. In fact, all plants have aspirin, and recently scientists have discovered they use it for fighting disease and stresses such as cold or drought. So an aspirin in a vase of cut flowers probably helps them fight infection and maybe prolongs their life.

Habitats of house plants

THE DOMESTIC CLIMATE

Did you know that your kitchen can be like a tropical rainforest, the hallway like the dark undergrowth on a spartan mountainside, and that a south-facing window compares to an Arizona desert? Homes have climates, varying from room to room, and even within a single room there are ecological 'niches' – hot or cool spots, well lit or shady.

We can never get the conditions in a home like the wild environments of house plants so it will always be a compromise, but the first thing is to appreciate the various climates in different rooms and how they change throughout the day and also throughout the seasons.

The trouble with our homes is that they are usually too dark and dry for most pot plants, but there are some good things to offset the problems. Coal fires, gas fires, pets and humans all give off the carbon dioxide which plants crave. The level of carbon dioxide is a hundred or even a thousand times higher indoors than outside. And the more carbon dioxide plants have the less water they need and the less roots they need to grow, so that more energy is put into growing shoots and flowers. That is one reason why house plants can stand being grown cramped in relatively small pots.

In the wild tropical rainforest homes of many of our common house plants, the air is thick with water moisture and humidity measures 70 to 80 per cent. But the average centrally heated home only has about 30 per cent humidity in winter, though it becomes a little higher in the summer when the heating is turned off. This is a big discrepancy, and unfortunately if we made things humid enough for our house plants the walls would be running with condensation, wallpaper peeling off, and carpets and furniture rotting. Unless you're a real plant fanatic it's simply unrealistic.

Acute problem spots can arise in rooms. Hot air from radiators, fridges and cookers can scorch foliage and dry out soil in pots. Cold draughts from windows are a problem during cold weather, especially at night when plants can be shut off by curtains from the warmth of the room. Cold draughts from doors, especially front and back doors, can also give a nasty cold shock to a nearby plant.

A house plant will usually appreciate being matched with the climate closest to its natural home. The living room is like a warm tropical, but dry, forest, and often turns into a desert. It is commonly heated to about 18 – 23°C (65 – 73°F) in winter, although heating is reduced at night, but as long as it does not fall below 13°C (55°F) most warmth-loving plants should survive, such as African violets, *Calathea, Maranta,* busy Lizzie, *Anthurium, Philodendron, Setcreasea, Tradescantia,* spider plant, *Zebrina, Spathiphyllum, Dieffenbachia,* Indian rubber plant, *Chamaedorea, Phoenix, Begonia,* Swiss cheese plant. The dangerous cold spots for these plants are windows and doors during winter, though double-glazing helps prevent windows from becoming freezing spots during cold nights.

The big problem, especially in centrally heated living rooms, is likely to be dry air. Tropical forest plants usually need humidity so extra moisture often needs to be given, and they need to be kept away from fires and radiators.

South-facing windows are ideal for succulents and flowering plants. Warmth-loving plants that tolerate shade are better kept away from living room windows.

Cooler rooms, such as dining rooms and bedrooms, can support plants capable of withstanding around 16°C (60°F) or less at night but the air will usually be more humid. Good examples of suitable plants are ivy, *Saxifraga stolonifera, Sparmannia africana, Begonia,* flowering bulbs.

The kitchen is sometimes the nearest to a jungle climate. It is usually warm, at least 18°C (65°F) day and night, and will probably get steamy from cooking and washing. So given adequate light or shade, quite delicate plants can be grown there, such as *Fittonia* and *Pilea* which must have high humidity. African violets often do well on shaded kitchen windowsills, and with full sun cacti and other succulents do well.

Bathrooms are humid places but if they are without central heating they are not usually too warm, 16 – 18°C (60 – 65°F), and light is usually poor because windows are small and frosted or rippled. These dark humid conditions are ideal for ferns and other heavy shade plants such as *Asplenium nidus, Cyperus, Ficus benjamina.*

Hall, stairs and landings are difficult places where it's draughty and dry; light varies a lot and there are occasional severe, cold draughts especially near the front door. Only the toughest plants survive these conditions, such as *Aspidistra, Sansevieria, Chlorophytum.*

Basements are usually cold, very dark, but humid – ideal for mushroom-growing but not much else!

Climates also vary during the day. Homes are usually colder during the night when the heating is turned off, but most plants can cope with a drop of a few degrees. The problems often come during cold winters, especially with wildly fluctuating temperatures between the day and night. Most house plants from the jungle find large swings of temperature a particular problem, but desert plants such as cacti are better suited to them. So bring in jungle plants at night from exposed places like windowsills where they run the risk of being chilled, or worst of all, frozen.

OUT IN THE WILD

So what was life like for house plants in their original wild homes?

Tropical forests – what we like to call jungles – are made up of layers: tall trees towering over smaller trees, over shrubs, over herb plants on the forest floor. These layers can be so thick they are like umbrellas, screening out both sun and rain. In fact, the different layers have different climates.

At the top of the canopy there is plenty of sun, wind and daily changes in humidity and temperature. But on the sheltered forest floor the air is still, humid, and the temperature is high but hardly varies. Many of the common house plants come from the rainforest floor because of their suitability for low light indoors.

This layered structure of the jungle is the key to understanding many of the requirements of house plants which came originally from there. The natural habitat of epiphytes, for instance, is high up in the tallest treetops in full sunlight where conditions are more like a desert than a forest, forcing the plants to endure periods of drought, intense sunlight and heat. So epiphytes tend to be good at going without watering for days on end, and enjoy bright sunshine.

Meanwhile, down on the forest floor things are very different. The treetops screen out so much light from the forest floor that plants living there are almost in total gloom. Only about four per cent of the sunlight falling on the treetops reaches the ground and comes down as sun flecks lasting a split second, otherwise there is a sort of greenish gloomy light diffused or bounced around through the leaves above. To add insult to injury, the treetops absorb most of the red and blue light needed for photosynthesis so that most of the light reaching the plants on the ground is of poor quality.

Yet despite this rather gloomy environment on the forest floor, the ground is covered in two types of plants: the seedlings of trees and climbers struggling to push up into the tree canopy above, many of which have special juvenile leaves adapted to the low light of the forest floor. The Swiss cheese plant is a classic climber. Its weedy looking seedling scampers across the forest floor in search of a tree to climb, then when it touches one it turns into a big robust twining stem with lush leaves and climbs up into the daylight above.

There are also plants that spend their whole existence in the gloom: dwarf trees such as the dwarf palms often found in South American and South-east Asian forests and soft-stalked (herb) plants such as the arrowroot family (Marantaceae) – fittonias, pileas and peperomias. Many of these herb plants have evolved into superb solar collectors to scavenge as much light as they can grab. They have broad leaves peppered with microscopic pimples which behave like lenses and filter light down inside the leaves, where the cells pipe the light, like fibre optics, down into the green

tissues where the photosynthesis is done. The undersides of the leaves are quite remarkable as well because they behave like mirrors – they are often coloured red which acts like the silver backing of a mirror, reflecting light back up into the leaf.

Another phenomenon of under-storey herbs in both tropical and temperate forests is mottling of the leaves with spots or blotches. One idea is that these marks may camouflage the plant from the eyes of herbivores. But the cost of camouflage is heavy, because white markings leave it with less area to photosynthesize.

The forest isn't all thick layers. Where old trees die the forest floor opens up to daylight, and along the banks of rivers and lakes where there is plenty of sunshine plants such as busy Lizzie and *Streptocarpus* thrive.

Another interesting thing about all rainforest plants is that their leaves very often taper to a downwardly pointing tip. The wetter the forest, the longer the tips. This is a plant drainage system. As rain pours down on the leaf it runs down the leaf veins, and off the tips. This is the way in which the plants avoid being choked. A film of water on their leaves would encourage infection as well as suffocate the 'breathing pores' which carry gas in and out of the leaf. Good drainage also helps avoid tiny lichens and algae settling on moist leaf surfaces and eventually covering them and shading the leaf.

Benefits of house plants

House plants aren't just pretty flowers and foliage – they also clean up pollution. Scientists have found that plants have an amazing knack of absorbing all sorts of fumes leaking out from glued wood joints, gas cookers, fires and all sorts of other domestic pollution. The plants seem to be able to absorb the fumes through the leaf pores and somehow fix the noxious gases inside. But different species of plant have different powers of absorption. Boston fern

(*Nephrolepis exaltata* 'Bostoniensis'),
Chrysanthemum morifolium and dwarf date
palm (*Phoenix roebelenii*) remove formaldehyde
(from new carpets and glued wood joints),
dwarf date palm cleans up xylene (from paints
and adhesives) and lady palm and yuccas have
the happy knack of getting rid of bathroom
smells because they absorb ammonia.

So good are house plants at absorbing
pollution, that a company in the United States
is now marketing a complete house plant kit
which cleans up all waste air and water from
homes and offices. Perhaps this explains why
house plants in offices tend to cut down
headaches and some of the other symptoms of
'sick building syndrome'.

House plants also cut down dust, fungi and
bacteria in the air. Many plants are coated with
a fine layer of wax on their leaves which is
continually replenished from special glands in
the leaf. The wax sticks airborne dirt on to the
leaf, and as new wax surfaces from the glands
the old wax sloughs off – rather like the wax in
our ears which does much the same job by
keeping dirt out!

So beware of washing leaves, especially with
detergents, because the waxy layer is easily
stripped off and leaves the plant dangerously
exposed to infection.

Plants are now well appreciated by town
planners for cutting down noise, and banks of
trees alongside roads reduce traffic noise
appreciably. Inside homes, house plants have
their own modest sound insulation, and a room
full of plants definitely lends a hushed
atmosphere to the place. Unfortunately they do
little to get rid of noisy neighbours.

There are a lot of people who swear that
house plants do something much more
mysterious – they make them feel better. It isn't
something physical, like cutting down
pollution, but more psychological, and it's very
difficult to pin down exactly. Some experts say
that having greenery around us – especially in
cities – reminds us of nature and the
countryside and makes us feel good. Also,
looking after plants is good therapy and relaxes
us. It's a fascinating subject but there are very
few scientific studies on it.

'POTTED' CUISINE
This isn't an area for experimentation: daffodil
sandwiches make you sick and cactus spines
cause complications, but pansy and pepper
quiche can be quite inviting. Edible flowers
have been eaten for centuries, and if you know
the right ones they can really spice up a boring
salad. Nasturtiums are quite a well-known
addition to salads, and in Guatemala white
flowers from the yucca are fried up with eggs. A
mature potted yucca will only rarely produce
these white bell-shaped flowers, so you might
have to wait a bit for that special breakfast. But
how about damask rose petal and lavender tart
for afters? Or if that's too fattening, some fruit
from the *Opuntia* cactus? The plants can be
grown outside on a patio in the summer and
can flower from May to June, being brought
indoors for the fruit to ripen in early winter.
The ripe fruit tastes like a tart blackberry with
red juice, but has to be carefully peeled to avoid
the cunningly persistent barbed spines
(glochids) which can cause a rash.

You don't have to butcher your house plants
for their flowers because you can get seasonal
mixed packets of edible blooms from top
supermarkets (*Gardening Which?* magazine for
May 1993 has a report on the subject).

Conservation and house plants
The thought of buying a plant pillaged from
the wild is a growing concern for many people.
The vast majority of plants are sold as
artificially propagated specimens, raised from
seed, cuttings or tissue culture techniques. Of
course, all the potted plants come from stock
that was originally collected from the wild, but
there are still two strong motivations for plants
to be collected from their natural habitat. The
first is that it is sometimes cheaper to import
wild selected stock rather than spend several

years bringing on large or slow-growing plants, and the second is the demand to supply the few collectors who still want to own rare wild-collected plants. Amid all the thousands of plants available, the difficulty for the pot plant owner is to know which are the wild-collected plants.

You can buy the majority of house plants with a completely clear conscience, but if in doubt when buying plants it is always worth asking questions about their origin. In general, garden centres have plants that all come from nursery-raised stock, but there are several groups of plants where this may not be the case, and it is worth asking about the following:

- ○ tropical orchids
- ○ unusual cacti and succulents such as aloes
- ○ bulb plants such as cyclamen
- ○ cycads, palms and tree ferns
- ○ carnivorous plants
- ○ air plants

Be suspicious of very large and unusual specimens of cacti; they may have been grown in this country but it is much cheaper for an importer to get wild-collected specimens than for them to have been grown for years in a nursery.

Plants such as the Venus flytrap are extremely vulnerable to collectors. The flytrap only lives in a small area of North Carolina, and although it grows in awesome numbers in the peaty sandbogs there, it could easily be wiped out of existence. Commercial collectors illegally have dug up tens of thousands of plants for garden centres worldwide and the fines are so small that they can afford to carry on.

But on the positive side, efforts are now under way to conserve some of the wild ancestors of house plants. One project is starting to collect a small royalty from house plants sold at garden centres and plough the money back into conservation, using an international network of botanic gardens. And hopefully, if this scheme proves successful, then all plants sold will eventually carry a conservation levy. After all, if animal conservation can raise huge sums to save interesting animals, why can't the same be done for plants?

A Potted History of House Plants

Why anyone should want to keep samples of obscure alien vegetation in their homes has never been fully explained. In many parts of the world it is still considered a very odd thing to do, especially when the plant you are keeping often grows like a weed in its native country. How about a nice pot of nettles for the kitchen windowsill? But certainly in the West, keeping plants in homes and offices is becoming ever more popular. In Holland, the biggest supplier of house plants in the world, the combined pot and cut plant industry is now worth over $2.5 billion a year. There is obviously more to our need for keeping house plants than meets the eye.

The idea of keeping plants in containers seems to have evolved from the development of ornamental gardens, the first of which were probably designed 5000 years ago for the palaces of the ancient Chinese civilization. Some sources suggest that potted herbs may have been grown by the ancient Egyptians over 3000 years ago. Certainly herbs which the Egyptians had at that time, such as fenugreek and coriander, are still grown as pot-herbs in countries such as Yemen. Even so, many of the plants that the Egyptians may have wanted for food or adornment grew wild or could be easily grown outdoors. The cornflowers, olive leaves and papyrus reeds illustrated in their hieroglyphic writing are all of cut plants. The mortuary temple of Queen Hatshepsut (c. 1470 BC) records that exotic plants were grown, such as frankincense trees from Oman and Somalia, but these were kept in gardens.

Yet if the Egyptians did not 'invent' the potted plant, they were certainly well on the way. From about 1800 BC some of the larger Egyptian houses had a central courtyard, in which there was a pool full of lotus waterlillies. Vines and trees in the courtyard were halfway to being potted because they had soil stacked around their trunks surrounded by a little hollow to contain the water.

Tutankhamun's tomb shows one of the first examples of what might be taken to be potted plants. When he died in 1327 BC a hollowed out container full of germinated cereal grains was buried with him. The container was in the shape of the cult god Osiris and was full of newly grown barley symbolizing life after death. They were known as 'Osiris beds' and adorned the tombs of people of high status.

Nebuchadnezzar, who built the hanging gardens of Babylon for his wife Amytis, may also have a claim to potted history. Twelve hundred years after the death of Tutankhamun he had designed fabulous terraced structures with deep brick trenches to hold the soil for large trees.

The Romans, spurred on by the lust to catch the beauty of the rose, were the first to grow plants indoors. They forced early blossoms by growing them in heated structures with thin sheets of the transparent mineral, mica, as the roof. In the time of emperor Nero, they cultivated a variety that was probably of the Damask rose, *Rosa damascena bifera*. They were sent to Rome in enormous quantities as part of a cut-flower trade. The Romans also grew herbs, decorative laurels and fruit trees in terracotta pots, but in the absence of big glass

Geraniums (*Pelargonium*) are tough plants from the arid bushlands of South Africa, so as house plants they make an excellent display on sunny windowsillls.

windows, the nearest they got to growing them indoors was in rooms with open ceilings, called atriums.

Potted herbs continued to be grown in European monasteries in the middle ages, and in the thirteenth and fourteenth centuries the art of forcing fruit under glass was very occasionally practised. In the sixteenth century, with the start of regular sea trade routes to the East, orange trees were brought to Holland and then to Britain. They were kept in tubs outside at first and only put indoors in heated sheds during the winter. In the 1670s glass orangeries were built for stately homes; they contained not only oranges but lemon, jasmine, olive, oleander and pomegranate.

Potted indoor plants proper did not appear in this country until the seventeenth century. One of the first was the cheerful *Campanula* from northern Italy, *Campanula pyramidalis* which was usually stood in an empty fireplace during the summer. In 1722 Thomas Fairchild published *The City Garden* in which he mentioned a number of more unusual plants such as aloes (which he said would grow well in London!) and the 'torch thistle', which was probably a type of mammillaria cactus.

The Victorians never did things by halves and it was they who were the past masters of the potted plant. The craze started off slowly with scented geraniums, chlorophytums, cacti and aloes. In a famous passage from *Dombey and Son* (1848) Charles Dickens writes about the plants in the window of Mrs Pipchin's front-parlour: 'There were half-a-dozen specimens of the cactus, writhing round bits of lath, like hairy serpents; another specimen shooting out broad claws, like a green lobster; several creeping vegetables, possessed of sticky and adhesive leaves; and one uncomfortable flower-pot hanging to the ceiling, which appeared to have boiled over, and tickling people underneath with its long green ends, reminded them of spiders'. It's fun to try to work out what all these plants were: the boiling pot may have been the spider plant, *Chlorophytum*, or the mother of thousands, *Saxifraga stolonifera*, the 'hairy serpents' the rat-tail cactus, *Aporocactus flagelliformis*, and it's possible that the carnivorous sundew was the creeping plant with sticky leaves.

A change in the plants the Victorians kept came about in the 1850s with the introduction of gas for lighting and cooking in the urban homes. Previously plants just got dirty from the coal fires, but now they died from the gas fumes. So hardier plants with tough thick leaves were added to the collection: aspidistras, rubber plants, spiny agave and certain palms.

In 1829, while keeping hawk moth pupae in a glass bottle, the naturalist Nathaniel Ward made an important and accidental discovery. On checking the moth cocoons several months after placing them in the bottle he found that a sprig of grass and a tiny fern were sprouting from a moist piece of earth that had fallen to the bottom. When he had tried to grow ferns in the past they had died in the foul London air,

but the bottled fern lived for half a year without water. He experimented with all sorts of bottles and glass tanks and in 1841 published a paper called 'Growth of Plants in Closely Glazed Spaces'. The original bottle became so famous that it was shown at the World's Fair in 1851. 'Wardian' glass cases caught on and allowed many more delicate and humidity-loving varieties such as the beautifully coloured caladiums, coleus, dracaenas, *Selaginella*, and a huge variety of ferns to beautify the home. The invention also revolutionized plant collecting because it allowed plants to be kept in good condition on the deck of a ship returning from long tropical expeditions.

A variation of the Wardian case was the miniature glass windowbox or *hortus fenestralis*,

Aspidistra was a favourite Victorian potplant because it copes well with neglect, pollution and shade.

a glass case set into the frame of a window, in which the plants were kept. As well as being an excellent place for the plants, it covered up any ugly views, a useful idea which could be reintroduced today!

Cheap glass from the 1850s onwards allowed many of the larger town houses to make conservatories. Many of our now familiar house plants were kept, as well as a few interesting species that have gone out of favour. Several of these species would be useful in our dry centrally heated houses today, such as the pony tail or *Beaucarnea*, and the palm-like shrub *Dasylirion*.

The Victorians also had fashions and crazes for various plants. There was a massive craze for keeping ferns, which some botanists have jokingly described as 'pteridomania' and a fashion for plants with coloured foliage leaves such as *Begonia rex*. This was started by the keeper of the botanical gardens in Paris who used sub-tropical bedding plants in a famous display at Parc Monceau. A craze for orchid collections later in the century made several species extinct in the wild.

The house plant pandemonium of the Victorian era cooled off in the early part of this century, but hundreds of new hybrids appeared of plants such as begonia, fuchsia, busy Lizzie and African violet. Interesting crosses were attempted such as that between the ivy (*Hedera*) and castor oil plant (*Fatsia*) to produce a beautiful foliage plant called *Fatshedera*, first marketed in 1912. In the 1930s the African violet rose to fame, and the post-war fifties saw house plants burgeon in many more homes with less sensitive hybrids that were easier to keep. New plants continue to appear, such as colourful *Chrysanthemum* and *Streptocarpus* hybrids as well as new leafy foliage plants like the *Radermachera*, introduced in the 1980s.

In the nineties, even in recession, there is still evidence that Britain is potty about house plants. According to the UK Flowers and Plants Association, on average we spend £19 each a year on plants, about a third on potted plants

Top of the Pots

In September 1993 these were the top ten groups in British House Plants, by value:

1. Flowering begonia
2. Large specimen foliage plants: *Ficus*, umbrella trees, palms, etc.
3. Ivies
4. Small foliage plants: *Ficus*, *Dieffenbachia*, crotons, etc.
5. Bottle garden plants: ivies, *Tradescantia*, *Dracaenas*, etc.
6. *Kalanchoe*
7. Pot chrysanthemums
8. African violets
9. Busy Lizzie 'New Guinea'
10. Miniature pot roses

(Compiled by the Flowers and Plants Association, London)

and the rest on cut flowers. That works out as a total of just over £1 billion on house plants and cut flowers. It's not as much as in northern European countries such as Norway, where the figure is £83 per year, but the market in Britain is increasing yearly by about 10 per cent in the past decade.

The Future

But rather than fuss over our plants and worry about their indoor climate, do we have the right sort of house plants in the first place? Many of our pot plants were introduced in the days when we lived in winter in damp, fairly cool homes with limited coal-fired heating. These days central heating is so common that the climate in our homes has shifted to a dry, hot environment, and you could say we should be growing more plants adapted to this climate. So some botanists are now looking for new plants from dry hot regions to bring back as house plants.

Suggested Plants for Your Home

To help you choose plants for each room in your house, here is a suggested list of the most appropriate plants to suit the likely conditions of the room. This is only a rough guide as room conditions in different houses will vary widely. To get more information on the plants you are interested in, turn to the alphabetized List of Plants on page 27.

Living rooms

Asplenium nidus (bird's nest fern)
Aloe – dry living room
Ananas comosus (pineapple) – sunny windowsill
Anthurium scherzerianum (flamingo flower) – bright bay window
Asparagus fern – bright/ slightly shaded living room
Aspidistra
Begonia

Begonia corallina de lucerna – fairly bright living room
BROMELIADS
Calathea
Ceropegia (Rosary plant, string of hearts)
Chlorophytum comosum (spider plant)
Ctenanthe – if humid enough
Dendrobium (see ORCHIDS)
Dieffenbachia (dumb cane) – half-shaded living room out of direct sunlight
Epipremnum – living room in moderate shade, humid and warm
Euphorbia pulcherrima (Poinsettia) – bright windowsill
Ficus benjamina (weeping fig) – a bright spot
Ficus elastica
Gardenia jasminoides (cape jasmine) – bright, warm and sunny living room

The air plants survive appalling hardship because they are adapted to living in hot, dry treetops in the tropics.

Gymnocalycium – sunny windowsill

Hedera (ivy) – light living room away from direct sun

Hippeastrum leopoldii (amaryllis) – bright living room windowsill

Hoya carnosa, hoya australis (wax plants) – bright, light bay window

Impatiens wallerana (busy Lizzie) – bright location in living room

Maranta (prayer plant)

Monstera deliciosa (Swiss cheese plant)

Pelargonium (geranium)

Philodendron – moderate shade

Phoenix (date palm)

Saintpaulia ionantha (African violet)

Sansevieria trifasciata (mother-in-law's tongue) – warm, dry living room

Schefflera (umbrella tree)

Setcreasea purpurea – warm, bright, light living room

Sparmannia africana – brightly lit place, especially bay window

Spathiphyllum (peace lily) – shady living room with high humidity

Tradescantia (spiderwort)

Zebrina pendula – moderate light away from a window

Dining rooms/ bedrooms

Aspidistra

Azalea/rhododendron

Begonia

Cyclamen persicum

Dracaena draco (dragon tree)

Cool, half-shaded rooms are ideal for flowering begonias, originally adapted to the shade of tropical forests.

Exacum affine

Ficus pumila (creeping or Chinese fig) – shady dining room (no direct sunlight)

Hedera (ivy)

Hyacinth orientalis – cool dark cupboard to start, then moderately cool bedroom

Jasminum (jasmine)

Narcissus (daffodil) – cool bright bedroom

Primula sinensis

Saxifraga stolonifera (mother of thousands)

Sparmannia africana

Kitchens

Aechmea fasciata (urn plant)

Adiantum (maidenhair fern) – warm, humid, shady

Aphelandra (zebra plant or saffron spike) – steamy kitchen

Cacti/succulents in full sun

Caladium (angel's wings)

Calathea

Codiaeum (croton)

Cordyline australis (cabbage palm)

Ctenanthe

Dionaea muscipula (Venus flytrap)

Fittonia (mosaic plant)

Guzmania

Maranta (prayer plant) – half-shaded humid places

Nephrolepis (ladder fern)

Peperomia (pepper elder)

Phalaenopsis (moth orchid)

Pilea cadierei

Saintpaulia ionantha (African violet) – steamy kitchen

Sarracenia (trumpet pitcher)

Vriesea

Zygocactus (Schlumbergera) (Christmas cactus)

Bathrooms

Adiantum (maidenhair fern)

Aphelandra (zebra plant or saffron spike)

Ctenanthe

FERNS
Ficus pumila – shady
   bathroom
Guzmania
Heavy shade plants
   e.g. *Asplenium nidus,*
   Cyperus, Ficus benjamina
Maranta (prayer plant)
Nephrolepis (ladder fern)
Saintpaulia ionantha (African
   violet) – steamy kitchen
Selaginella martensii
Spathiphyllum (peace lily)
Streptocarpus
Syngonium podophyllum
   (goosefoot)
Tradescantia (spiderwort)
Vriesea

Warm rooms

Euphorbia milii (crown of
   thorns) – almost anywhere
   dry and hot
Passiflora caerula (passion
   flower)
Phoenix (date palm)
Platycerium (stag's horn fern)
Streptocarpus – humid

Cool rooms

Cyclamen
Crocus
Dracaena draco (dragon tree)
Fatshedera – cool, shady or
   light rooms
Rosa chinensis minima (pot
   roses)
Primula sinensis
Tulip

Bring a touch of *Jurassic Park* to
your bathroom! Ferns are ancient
plants, many of them adapted to
shady, humid forest floors.

Hall, stairs and landings

Aspidistra
Azalea/rhododendron
Chlorophytum
Cyclamen
Dracaena draco (dragon tree)
Radermachera sinica/
  Stereospermum suaveolens
  e.g. entrance hallway but
  must be in bright location
Sansevieria (mother-in-law's
  tongue)

Conservatories

Arisaema triphyllum (Jack-in-
  the-pulpit)
Dicksonia and Cyathea (tree
  ferns)
Phalaenopsis (moth orchid)
Phyllitis scolopendium (hart's
  tongue fern)

Basement flats/ shady rooms

Begonia rex
Begonia tuberhybrida
Chrysalidocarpus

Sunny windowsills

Astrophytum (cactus)
BROMELIADS/ *Tillandsia* –
  bright sunny window
Callisia
Codiaeum (croton)

LEFT Conservatories are good for
large sun-loving plants such as
Sparmannia, tree ferns and
Ferocactus.
RIGHT Special shade plants like
lady palm and *Aspidistra* are ideal
for shady corners.

Darlingtonia (cobra lily)
Drosera (sundews)
Ferocactus (barrel cactus)
Gymnocalycium
Hibiscus rosa-sinensis – east- or
  west-facing windowsill
Hippeastrum (Amaryllis) –
  living rooms
Kalanchoe (flaming Katy)
Lithops (stone plant) – south-
  or west-facing window
Mammillaria
Pilea cadierei (aluminium plant)
  – not in direct sunlight

Bottle gardens

Fittonia verschaffeltii (mosaic
  plant)
Phyllitis scolopendium (hart's
  tongue fern)
Selaginella martensii

Porches

Hydrangea macrophylla – cool,
  sunny position

Almost anywhere

Aspidistra
Asplenium nidus (bird's nest
  fern)
Chamaedorea elegans (parlour
  palm)
Chlorophytum comosum (spider
  plant)
Chrysanthemum
Ficus elastica (India rubber
  plant)
Rhapis excelsa (lady palm)
Yucca elephantipes – needs
  good light

A Brief Glossary

We have tried to keep botanical or horticultural jargon to the very minimum, but here are a few terms that might come in useful.

Bulbs A fleshy, juicy underground shoot used for overwintering in plants such as hyacinth and tulip. New plants can be grown from side bulbs which develop from the main bulb.

Corm A short swollen underground shoot used for overwintering in plants such as crocus and Venus flytrap. By the end of the growing season the main corm has withered, but new side corms have developed which can be broken off and repotted to grow into new plants.

Epiphytes Plants that grow on trees or other objects for support, and out of touch with the ground, but they do *not* suck out juices from the trees like a parasite.

Floral bracts Modified leaves which surround the flower proper, but which in some species, such as the poinsettias, are very obvious and coloured in their own right.

Glochids On cacti, patches of barbed bristles that hook into the skin and cause irritation; found especially on *Opuntia*.

Plantlets Small plants formed on the mother plant. These can break off and when grown in the right conditions lead independent lives, for example, some kalanchoes.

Propagation Growing new plants, either by sexual propagation using the seeds from fertilized flowers, or by vegetative propagation using leaf, stem, root or other sorts of cuttings.

Prothallus A minute leaf which develops from the spore of a fern. It holds the sex cells on its surface which will fuse and produce a new spore-bearing fern.

Raceme A group of flowers with a central stem that has blooms at intervals.

Rhizomes An underground stem which grows horizontally. It is used by the plant for overwintering and for spreading outwards and growing new plants.

Spathe A coloured or green hood partly covering the spadix in aroids; a type of petal-like bract or modified leaf.

Spadix A slender and often pitted flower spike found in aroids, partly surrounded by the spathe.

Succulent Fleshy stems and leaves in plants growing in arid lands, used for storing water and food during droughts.

Variegation Patterns of colours or shades of a leaf or flower.

List of Plants

The plants featured here include some of the commonest house plants as well as some interesting exotics that are becoming more popular, such as bromeliads and carnivorous plants.

    The plants are listed alphabetically, usually under the generic name, but main entries are sometimes given under the common name, depending on popular usage. In these cases the generic name is cross-referenced to the main entry. There are also some interesting groups of plants, such as cacti and aroids, which have been given their own headings and descriptions.

Adiantum
See Maidenhair fern

Aechmea fasciata
[Urn plant]

See also BROMELIADS

Aechemea fasciata is a bromeliad from the mountain forests of Latin America, growing on trees in a relatively cool, misty climate. But even though it is used to cool conditions, grown as a house plant it does not like to be kept too cold, and temperatures of less than about 10°C (50°F) are risky.

    The urn plant gets its name from the way its leaves are pressed together into an urn or funnel shape which collects rain-water in the wild. This water tank helps the plant through patchy droughts which is one of the hazards of being perched up in the trees. So indoors the house plant needs only moderate watering but the leaf cup needs topping up with fresh water.

    There is also very little soil on the trees, so the urn plant has a very modest root system and

as a house plant it needs only a small pot. Or for a more natural appearance, it can be fixed to a mossy pole, similar to the way it grows in the wild, by taking the plant out of its pot, wrapping the base of the plant in moss or large bits of fibrous coir and lightly binding the whole bundle with nylon fishing-line. The whole plant can then be attached to a mossy pole using plastic-covered wire.

    Aechmeas have a variety of stunning blooms, from blue to yellow, and they can flower all the year round. But sadly after flowering the plant dies, although you can easily propagate baby plants from the main plant. Two new plantlets

---

PLANTS *Aechmea fasciata*
REGION OF ORIGIN Tropical and sub-tropical Latin America
WILD HABITAT Treetops in mountain areas
HOME HABITAT Bright rooms with humidity, e.g. kitchens
COMMON PROBLEMS Too cold a position causes leaf rot and leaf damage; cold water and waterlogging can also cause rot

form at either side of the leaf rosette base and these can be broken off and potted once they have started growing their own roots. Alternatively you can leave them on the parent plant which will wither away, leaving two new plants. They will take about four years to come into flower, but that can be shortened by at least a year by attaching the bromeliad to a mossy pole.

There are about 150 species of aechmeas, and although many of them make good house plants, *Aechmea fasciata* is by far the most popular.

African violet

[*Saintpaulia ionantha*]

African violets are the most popular house plants in the world: over 200 million are sold worldwide each year. Yet ironically they may be facing extinction in their native homes of Tanzania and Kenya. They now have only one stronghold left, in the forests of the Usambara

Saintpaulia ionantha

Mountains, in northern Tanzania. Intense farming and some illegal logging in the surrounding area is threatening even this last refuge, but conservation bodies and the Tanzanian government are working to improve yields from existing land to relieve pressure on the virgin forest.

There are at least twenty species of *Saintpaulia* but *Saintpaulia ionantha* was the first one discovered and was the main stock from which our hybrids were made. It is a blue flowered plant, and although the other species look very similar to it there are variations in the number of flowers, and in the hairiness and length of the leaves.

African violets in the wild have plenty of moisture. They grow on steep rocky banks protected by the warm, humid shade of the trees above. *Saintpaulia ionantha* comes from the lowlands near the coast where moisture from sea mists rolls in from the Indian Ocean. The leaves absorb the moisture by means of their fine hairs. There are also wet seasons in this part of East Africa too, when it can rain non-stop for several weeks. Yet strangely one of the commonest ways of killing these plants in the home is overwatering them. Why?

One of the important features of the African violet's wild home is that it grows on rocks, in thin patches of soil, and usually at an angle. So the rain drains off the leaves and roots very quickly and the plants don't become waterlogged. But as house plants, they are usually cooped up in small plastic pots with poor drainage, overwatered and even stood in water, and water often spills on to their leaves which makes them rot. So it is much safer to water the plants under their leaves or stand them in a saucer of water for just half an hour – they will need watering about once a week in a warm room during the summer, and monthly when it gets colder.

African violets need to be kept humid; one of the reasons they die in the wild is because protective trees above them have been logged, allowing their habitat to dry out. In the home

Wild African violets lead a shady, humid life sheltering under forests in Tanzania with little soil and good drainage.

they can be kept humid by standing them on a moist tray of wet pebbles in a shallow dish of water and letting the leaves absorb the moisture – in fact, you can let the roots dry out provided the leaves are kept very humid. Another way is to use a mister to keep them humid, but take care the misted leaves are not exposed to sunlight otherwise they will scorch.

African violets were discovered by a German provincial governor, Baron Saint Paul-Illaire (from whom they got their Latin name *Saintpaulia*). He found them growing outside caves among boulders in fissures and pockets filled with humus, with trees growing overhead. So African violets do not need much in the way of either soil or light. They are shade plants, adapted to catching flecks of sunlight passing

through the treetops, living in the diffuse shade of the trees' leaves. In strong sunlight they develop brown leaves and flowers. So if you stand them on a table in the middle of a room they'll be happy for a few weeks but then the flowers become pale and new flowers fail to bloom. What they love is 12 hours of diffuse daylight each day, just as they would get in the tropics, and then they start flowering in the home. On short, dark wintry days in the temperate world the natural daylight can be supplemented using artificial plant 'grow lamps' readily available from electrical shops, or fluorescent lights used close to the plants (not more than 20 cm (8 in) away). But once the flower buds have started growing, the flowers will come into bloom whatever the lighting

PLANTS *Saintpaulia ionantha*
REGION OF ORIGIN Tanzania
WILD HABITAT Rocky banks, slightly shaded, humid
HOME HABITAT Steamy kitchen, bathroom, or a humid spot in a living room not in sunlight
COMMON PROBLEMS Too much water on leaves causes rot; lack of flowers from poor light; blotches on leaves from sunlight burning through water droplets on the leaves

conditions, and they can flower all the year round as they would in the wild, although there is a concentration of the blooms at the start of the rainy season.

In their natural homes they are also used to a fairly constant warmth. So in the house they appreciate being kept at between 10–25°C (50–77°F). A useful guide is that if you feel warm and comfortable then so does the African violet. The big danger is that if the temperature drops to near freezing they collapse. So be careful not to water them with freezing cold water; use tepid water instead.

African violets have the reputation of being difficult plants to keep at home, which is probably one reason so many of them are sold – because they die so easily! But provided they are kept warm, given plenty of humidity and are kept away from direct bright sunlight they will do well. For instance, put them in a steamy kitchen or bathroom, standing the plants in shade in summer and on a sunny windowsill during winter (but be careful not to leave them there at night behind a curtain where it gets very cold unless there is double glazing).

If African violets grow too big for their pots they can be repotted in the spring. And if you are feeling adventurous you could try growing *Saintpaulia* in more natural conditions by making an indoor rockery with two or three large moss-covered stones on a big pebble tray, placing the plants in a little peat-based soil between some cracks.

Air plants
See *Tillandsia*

Aloe

Aloes are slow-growing succulent (fleshy) plants from the dry rocky bush regions of southern Africa and Madagascar, growing from coastal plains to mountainsides, often experiencing cool periods, but without frost.

There is a wide variety of aloes, most often with stemless rosettes, but there are also aloes with stems, the tree aloes. One of the most popular house plant species is *Aloe variegata*, with upright stripy leaves from the Cape Province of South Africa. It lives in the shade of bushes, so it doesn't appreciate strong sunlight in the home.

Another commonly kept aloe is *Aloe aristata*. It is more widespread in southern Africa than *A. variegata*, and tolerates a range of very arid habitats. It has light green leaves with little white warts or teeth on the surface, a wonderful orange or red flower stalk which appears on mature potted specimens, and it produces lots of offsets around its base.

Like all succulents, aloes are used to growing in seasons. Their wild bushland homes have a short wet winter and a dry summer with an average 40 cm (16 in) of rain per year, but the house plant actually needs the opposite: a good soaking when its soil dries out during the summer and a dry winter. The reason for the difference from its wild conditions is because of our light: in summer it grows in the long hours of bright light and without it the plant becomes straggly with an unnaturally elongated stem. But during the winter the light is so poor that it stops growing and needs to rest in a cool dry place. The cool part is important because although aloes die in freezing temperatures, temperatures of around 5°C (41°F) help to boost flowering the next season.

The great thing about looking after aloes is that because they come from dry places they easily enjoy the dry air in our homes. But be careful of their watering because they do not like being watered on their leaves, which can rot at their bases. Since the bases are tucked away out of sight you will not notice the rot setting in until the leaves begin to yellow and the plant starts to smell. At this point all the leaves start to fall out when they are touched. So it's really important to water the soil without wetting the leaves. If the leaves of your aloes turn crispy brown, then the soil needs a little water, but some species of aloe retain their dead brown leaves as a defence against fire by acting as a shield to protect the living leaves, such as *Aloe ferox*, a tall-stemmed aloe. When grown as a house plant the dead leaves should only be removed when totally crisp, and when there is no resistance to pulling them off.

Aloes propagate well, although this has little relevance to their wild habitats. Cuttings and

PLANTS Aloe
REGION OF ORIGIN Southern Africa, Madagascar
WILD HABITAT Bushlands, in shaded dry scrub
HOME HABITAT South-facing window but not directly in sun, particularly good for dry living rooms
COMMON PROBLEMS Water on leaves causes base rot; watering during winter can rot the plants; straggly growth in low light

offsets should root easily, but they need to be dried for a few days before putting into a very lightly watered sandy compost. Leaf cuttings must include the whole base of the leaf, if they are 'tidied up' by trimming off the whitish growing area, called the cambium, the cuttings will not root.

Humans first carried aloes from Africa to the Mediterranean and into Asia. They eventually became a sacred plant of Muslims, who hang aloe leaves over doors after a pilgrimage to Mecca to show that they have made the journey.

Aloes are also used commercially in shampoos, medicated soaps and creams. *Aloe vera* in particular has been used for centuries as a balm for minor burns and is a good plant to keep as a first aid on a kitchen windowsill. When the leaf is broken it oozes a clear, gooey sap and when this is applied to the scald it soothes and helps heal the wound. This is a well-known folklore remedy and recent scientific studies now reveal that aloes do indeed contain therapeutic chemicals which help prevent wounds from becoming painfully inflamed and swollen.

Not entirely recommended is the use of raw aloes for purging the bowels. Next to medicinal rhubarb, some species of aloe are the best thing for making you go. Alexander the Great once sent collectors to the island of Socotra to obtain laxative aloes. That was in 325 BC and people are still worried about their bowels.

Aloe nobilis

Aluminium plant

See *Pilea cadierei*

Amaryllis

See *Hippeastrum*

Ananas comosus

[Pineapple]

See also BROMELIADS

Pineapple grows wild in the sub-tropical and tropical Americas, and is grown commercially all over the tropics. But it is a bromeliad, just like the urn plant and is now becoming a popular house plant as well. *Ananas comosus* is the edible agricultural species, growing to about 90 cm (3 ft) in the tropics. The indoor plants are often a variegated variety of *A. comosus*, but unless it is grown in perfect sunny and humid conditions, as in a greenhouse, the pineapple will not fruit. The other available species is *Ananas bracteatus*, the red pineapple, which does sometimes fruit in the home. It comes from southern Brazil, where only the young fruits are eaten.

Unusually for bromeliads, pineapples grow on the ground in clumps, so they don't like being wired to moss poles or mock tree stumps. But like other wild cup bromeliads, their spiny-leaved rosette collects rain-water in its centre, which evaporates in the tropical heat and is then replenished by daily rains. But if the cup is kept full in the home then rot soon sets in, and what is really needed is a good soaking followed by drying off, as in the natural habitat. This can be done by watering the cup and then turning the whole pot at an angle of about 45° to let the water dribble out and run over the rosette. The plant also enjoys a thorough watering in its pot when the soil dries out during the summer growing season.

Like all bromeliads the parent plant dies back after flowering but fresh shoots growing from the bottom of the rosette can be broken off and potted as new plants, though these offsets will probably need heat from a propagator at about 20°C (68°F) to make roots. In large pots (40–60 cm) the plantlets, or 'pups' as they are sometimes called, can be left on the parent plant, which is carefully removed when it has died away. This method will slowly produce an attractive clump as each successive generation produces pups.

There is another and rather interesting way of propagating the plant – simply chop off the top of a pineapple fruit with a good head of leaves, and plant in a sand and peat fibre compost, cover with plastic and leave in a warm place. In the olden days, pineapples used to be grown like this in Britain in covered pits of rotting manure and compost – the heat of the rotting compost kept the plants warm and nourished all through the winter.

Pineapples are good house plants for keeping in bright sunny living rooms on a windowsill, and the stripy markings of the variegated varieties will flourish the more sun they get. They don't seem to mind dry air, but be careful of the serrated edges to the leaves which can easily cut curtains or skin. If you're really lucky, a healthy specimen may reward you with your very own pineapple fruit which grows out as a sideshoot from the leaf rosette, but this is rare.

Ananas is not a Latin or Greek name, but comes from the South American Indians who were probably growing pineapples before the arrival of the Spanish in the sixteenth century.

PLANTS *Ananas comosus*
REGION OF ORIGIN Sub-tropics and tropics of the Americas
WILD HABITAT On the ground in tropical rainforest
HOME HABITAT Sunny windowsill in living room; in dry rooms benefits from a damp pebble tray
COMMON PROBLEMS Lack of light leading to poor growth and lack of colours; stale water in central cup causes rot, as can overwatering in general

Angel's Wings
See *Caladium*

Anthurium
[Flamingo flower]
See also AROIDS

Anthurium is a genus of a forest plant of over 500 species, found all over tropical America and the West Indies, so they don't like to be kept cool (below about 10°C (50°F)) in the home. They are aroids, with a typical bloom made up of a leafy spathe and poker-shaped spadix which carries the flowers. The frequency of flowering depends on the variety grown, but 'Amazone' is a very good variety, producing lots of pink spathes throughout the growing season.

Some anthuriums are climbers and a few form clumps on the ground. They all enjoy high humidity, and it is so moist in their natural habitat that they don't need to produce many roots. In the home, creating a moist atmosphere is a top priority.

Anthurium is usually grown for its bright scarlet or red spathes which look like waxy, plastic plates. These advertise the curly inflorescences to insect pollinators. Those of *A. scherzerianum*, the most popularly kept clump-forming species, are available with red, dark red, pink, pink/spotted and white spathes.

Our winter light is so poor that the plant needs bright light, but not full sun, and during the summer it enjoys early morning and late evening sunlight without direct light in the middle of the day. During the growing season these plants love misting until it starts to run off their leaves but because of their epiphytic habit, the roots of the pot plant need good aeration by making the soil from a mix of coarse leaf mould or coir and peat. This in turn means that the soil doesn't have enough plant food in it, and so fortnightly liquid feeds are a good idea throughout the summer. The compost needs to be kept moist with tepid

PLANTS *Anthurium scherzerianum*
REGION OF ORIGIN Tropical America and the West Indies
WILD HABITAT Damp tropical forest, growing in clumps
HOME HABITAT Bright bay window facing north or east
COMMON PROBLEMS Not enough light leads to soft yellow leaves; sudden temperature changes bring about leaf drop; lack of humidity leads to brown and wrinkled leaves and the plant definitely benefits from standing in a damp pebble tray.

water, and the plant enjoys a damp pebble tray beneath its pot as well as its regular misting. Even so, to encourage flowering the next season, it's worth easing off the watering for several weeks during the winter.

Anthurium lives in shade or dappled sunlight, and makes the most of poor light by using 'lenses' on its leaf surface which focus light into the leaf interior to boost its photosynthesis. Many shade plants like this also

Anthurium scherzerianum

use 'fibre optics' in the cells inside their leaf to reflect light down to the photosynthezing cells. Their chloroplasts – the minuscule bodies inside the cells which actually do the photosynthesis – can even move inside the cells like primitive amoebae to catch the best light.

Aphelandra
[Zebra plant or saffron spike]

This is a genus of about twenty species of bushy plants from Mexico to southern Brazil. The household varieties are easily recognized by their yellow spike made up of bracts through which the flowers peep. They flower for about two months in the autumn, but are still interesting throughout the year because of the ivory veins on the leaves.

Aphelandra squarrosa is one of the most commonly grown species and comes from the rainforests of the southern Amazonia region where it gets regular soakings and a constantly high humidity. So in the home these conditions have to be replaced by misting and standing the pot on a damp pebble tray in a warm place (minimum of about 12°C, 54°F). The plant grows up to 1 m (3 ft) tall, although smaller varieties are available, such as 'Louisae' and 'Brockfeld'. There is also a red-flowering species called *Aphelandra aurantica*.

Since they are bushy plants aphelandras soon start to outgrow their pots, but it is possible to cut the plants down to their lower leaves, and then use the cut shoots and side branches for

---

PLANTS *Aphelandra squarrosa, A. aurantica*
REGION OF ORIGIN Tropical Latin America
WILD HABITAT Bushes of humid tropical rainforest
HOME HABITAT Steamy kitchen, bathroom, not in sunlight
COMMON PROBLEMS Dryness, so use mister or damp pebble tray; cold shock from sudden temperature change

---

propagating by rooting them in a plastic bag which will keep them warm and moist. An airy compost should be used, made from a mixture of coarse fibred coir or peat and vermiculite.

The plant should grow vigorously if kept well watered and misted in the summer, so it is a good idea to repot the *Aphelandra* each spring and feed weekly with a standard liquid feed such as those made from a seaweed extract.

Areca
See *Chrysalidocarpus*

Arisaema triphyllum
[Jack-in-the-pulpit]

See also AROIDS

Arisaema is an aroid with a typical bloom made up of a beautiful hooded spathe shielding a slim poker-shaped spadix and flowering in late spring and early summer. It has a single thick stem that sometimes has wine coloured stains and there are usually only one or two long stalked leaves on the plant which grow on the ground from a rhizome. Unlike some other aroids they are not tree climbers.

Arisaema comes from eastern Africa, India, Japan, China and Malaysia. In India it grows in the dappled light of the Western Ghat forest and scrubland, which has an evenly spread high annual rainfall. So the house plant needs plenty of light – but not direct midday and early afternoon sunlight – in a warm position, away from draughts (temperatures lower than 5–10°C (40–50°F) should be avoided), and coming from a humid environment it enjoys a daily spraying with a mister.

Plants in the *Arisaema* genus have been over-collected in the wild, so it is worth making sure that they are nursery grown. They can be grown from mature seed and offsets.

Arisaema blooms are normally male or female. In its first year of existence the plant is usually male, but as it gets larger it changes into a female. This sex change can even be

PLANTS *Arisaema triphyllum*
REGION OF ORIGIN East Africa and Asia
WILD HABITAT Damp tropical forest, growing from rhizome
HOME HABITAT Conservatory, bright bay window
COMMON PROBLEMS Not enough light causes spindly growth; sudden temperature changes can lead to leaf yellowing and death

A group of aroids

artificially induced by growing plants under dry, poor conditions, turning it male, or using a very rich environment to turn it female. This strategy makes sense in the wild. Under poor conditions, producing seeds and fruits can drain a plant of resources to the point of death. On the other hand, a male only makes relatively 'cheap' pollen and is more likely to survive, as well as making a vital contribution to cross-fertilization.

AROIDS

[Cheese plants, peace lilies, philodendrons]

From the tropical jungles of the world, aroids are some of the most peculiar plants you can grow indoors. In some species they have glorious leaves slashed or punctured into bizarre shapes like no other group of plants. And their blooms are also unusual: they all have a phallic-like poker sticking up from a large coloured bract called a spathe. Sometimes the spathe is a brightly coloured plate, as in *Anthurium*, or an elaborate cornet-shaped wrapper as in *Arisaema*. And many of the blooms play an amazing piece of deception on insects: the spadix and spathe imitate the colour and smell of rotting meat or faeces. Midges and flies think they have found food, fly down into the bloom and inadvertently pollinate the flowers at the bottom of the spadix.

In some cases the bloom even *heats up* like a rotting piece of detritus to attract the insect pollinators. In *Philodendron* the temperature rises up to 15°C (59°F) higher than the surrounding air. This is an astonishing piece of behaviour for any plant to perform, and scientists scratched their heads for years trying to find out how the plant heated up. What they discovered revealed a completely new feature of plants we knew nothing about before.

The *Philodendron* heat is made rather like the way we burn off calories during aerobic exercise. The poker and sterile male flowers in the bloom are full of fat and when they respire the fat is burnt off as heat. But that isn't the end of the story, because the heat is only turned on for just a few days of the year when the flowers are ready for pollination. So how does the bloom know when to heat up? The answer is truly astonishing: a surge of aspirin inside the plant turns on the floral heater.

We've known for many years that plants have aspirin – the bark of willow trees is so full of aspirin it was used for hundreds of years to treat headaches. But the aroids showed for the first time that aspirin in plants behaves like a hormone. And from that discovery, scientists then discovered that *all* plants use aspirin – not to heat up, but to help fight off diseases and perhaps toughen them against stresses such as drought and cold weather. All of which makes plausible the old folklore that putting an aspirin in a vase of cut flowers keeps them fresh.

Foraging aroids

Many aroids are climbing plants superbly adapted to finding and clinging on to trees. Yet their seedlings are often puny little white threads with a few tiny leaves. They crawl across the forest floor in search of shadows which tell them if they are getting close to a tree. But as soon as they touch a tree they go through an astonishing transformation, turning into thick twining stems which wrap themselves around the tree, climbing upwards in search of light. The stems also sprout luscious fleshy leaves, and as they mature the leaves start to rip apart into the familiar aroid shapes, like the holes of the Swiss cheese plant.

As the aroid climbs upwards it grows thirsty for more water and minerals, and the stem sprouts special roots which grow down to the ground below and plumb into the soil for nourishment. At the tops of trees some types of aroids also fire off special whip-like stems which cascade down to the ground searching for new trees to climb. And so the aroid slowly 'roams' through the forest crawling up trees and then dropping down again like some sort of green snake searching for daylight.

Going to so much effort to climb trees pays off in the long run, because the aroid saves itself all the time and energy of growing a woody trunk like a tree. Instead, it 'cheats' by cadging a lift from trees to reach the sunlight. It doesn't harm the trees apart from crowding out the trees' leaves. But exactly how foraging plants can suddenly switch from the seedling growth to the climbing habit is still a mystery.

AROIDS included in this book:

Anthurium	*Philodendron*
Arisaema triphyllum	*Spathiphyllum*
Caladium	Swiss cheese plant
Dieffenbachia	(*Monstera deliciosa*)
Epipremnum	*Syngonium*

Asparagus
[Asparagus ferns]

House plants of the *Asparagus* genus are mainly from South Africa but they are also found in the wild in East Africa, Madagascar, many of the islands of the Indian ocean, Sri Lanka and Australia. They have small flowers with red berries. The edible asparagus is a cultivated form of a wild European variety. Although they are not ferns, some species look very fern-like and because they come from drier habitats are great as fern substitutes in drier houses.

A lot of the species come from the sub-tropical bush scrub around the south-western Cape Province of South Africa. Here they grow among succulents such as the aloes, and are accustomed to dry warm summers (average 20°C (68°F)) and wet mild winters (average 12°C (54°F)). One adaptation to these dry conditions is their fleshy roots with fat tubers which can store water for short periods, so when they are grown as house plants it isn't a disaster if you occasionally forget to water them and their soil dries out between waterings. On the other hand, they do lose a lot of water through their

---

Asparagus umbellatus

PLANTS *Asparagus plumosus,
A. asparagoides* etc.
REGION OF ORIGIN Southern and eastern
Africa, Madagascar
WILD HABITAT Bushlands among dry scrub,
like aloe
HOME HABITAT Bright or slightly shaded
living room
COMMON PROBLEMS Rot through
overwatering; yellowing from too much sun or
extreme dryness

leaves in summer so at that time they appreciate plenty of watering, and if they become really stressed their leaves drop off. But they are also used to a winter season in the wild when their growth slows down, so it is worth easing off watering during our winters.

Potted asparagus grow well in a soil-based potting mixture, much better than in their wild habitat, and also benefit from feeding with a standard plant fertilizer about twice a month during the summer growing season.

A good location in the house is a bright living room though it can tolerate some shade but not direct sunlight.

The popular species, such as *Asparagus plumosus*, also known as *A. setaceus* or lacefern, is probably more familiar as part of a cut-flower display or as a buttonhole adornment. The feathery 'leaves' are not leaves at all, but modified branches called phylloclades, and with a magnifying glass you can see that they are covered in scales which are the true leaves. There are flat-leaved species too like *A. asparagoides* or smilax (syn. *A. medeoloides*), from the Cape of Good Hope. It is a vigorous climber and winds itself around any thin supports. Generally a mature asparagus holds itself up and 'climbs' over itself, using numerous small thorns along its branches, which can be very sharp and should be avoided.

Asparagus can be propagated by seed or by dividing the clump of an overcrowded pot, but this latter method has no relevance to its life in the wild.

Aspidistra

This is a native of large areas of China, Japan, Taiwan and the East Himalayas where it grows in the cool and often dense shade of mountain forests. Because of its tough lifestyle in the wild, the *Aspidistra elatior* coped well with life in Victorian homes: dim, cold rooms and the fumes from coal fires and gas lamps which killed most other plants – hence its common name, the cast-iron plant. Indeed, the aspidistra became a symbol of Victorian life, but it also attained the reputation that many people had given to the Victorians: stiflingly prudent and lack-lustre. George Orwell wrote about them with this theme in mind in *Keep the Aspidistra Flying*, about a man who was extremely careful about overspending. The aspidistra has since gone out of fashion because of its dullness, but that's a shame because it's one of the few house plants you can grow almost anywhere: in bathrooms, bedrooms, hallways, kitchens and living rooms, provided it is kept watered and out of direct sunlight. It can stand considerable neglect, but two things it cannot tolerate are waterlogging, and dry air causing brown leaves and helping infestations of red spider mites. The presence of these mites is recognized by a speckled yellowing of the whole leaf together with a dusty appearance on its underside, which is slightly sticky to the touch. If you stare at the underside of the leaf for long enough you will see the mites crawling quite fast over the surface, but as they are smaller than bread-crumbs it would be better to use a magnifying glass.

The dusty appearance is due to their droppings, shed mite skins and their eggs. Luckily they cannot reproduce in damp conditions so just misting the underside of the leaves regularly is a good way to get rid of them. For persistent attacks chemical sprays are commercially available, or you could try a weak solution of washing-up liquid in a spray.

A more interesting and environmentally friendly way of controlling the red spider mite

> **PLANTS** *Aspidistra elatior*
> **REGION OF ORIGIN** Eastern Asia
> **WILD HABITAT** Dense, cool mountain forests
> **HOME HABITAT** Almost anywhere, but tough enough to survive hallways, stairs, landings and other cool, draughty, shady areas (usually environments hostile to most other house plants!)
> **COMMON PROBLEMS** Dry air causing brown leaves and helping infestations of red spider mites; scorched in direct sunlight; probably the main cause of death is waterlogging the soil during winter

is to use its natural predator, *Phytosalis.* These minute creatures, which are another type of mite, are commercially available on leaves in a plastic tube. The leaves are taken out and put on the infested plant where they proceed to munch away on the red spider mites. When the spider mites have all been eaten the helpful *Phytosalis* will all starve to death so there should always be some infested plants in the house for the predator to feed on – for future insurance! A more recent use of the natural predator is to hang bags of them on the infected leaves.

A large part of the attraction of the *Aspidistra* is its big leaves, which are tough and evergreen for a special reason. Because the plant lives in soil very poor in nitrogen, it takes an enormous effort to grow big leaves. So the plant hangs on to its leaves as long as possible to protect its nitrogen investment. Even so, a monthly liquid feed does promote growth in the growing season, even though the plant would never get a fertilizer like this in the wild. But because of its spartan habits, aspidistras in the home can survive in very cramped pots and need repotting only every four to five years, in the spring; in fact, too much repotting can actually kill the plant.

Aspidistra is thought to have one of the oddest pollinators in the plant world. It grows lurid purple, but small, cup-shaped flowers produced at ground level and believe it or not

snails are thought to pollinate the flowers, which makes a change from snails eating plants. Sadly, even a well-kept plant will rarely produce these flowers in the home.

Asplenium

See also FERNS

Asplenium ferns are a worldwide genus with about 650 members and a wide variety of habitats. Some are tropical and intolerant of cool temperatures less than 18°C (64°F) and some are from cooler regions and can easily survive temperatures 5–7°C (40–45°F). *Asplenium scolopendrium*, the European hart's tongue fern, is a hardy species ideal for unheated rooms and has several ornamental varieties such as 'Crispum'. A warmth-loving *Asplenium* is the elegant *A. bulbiferum*, which has finely divided leaves like a carrot top. It comes from humid tropical or temperate forests in Australia, New Zealand, and southern Asia. The plant has an amazing power to propagate itself by growing 'babies' on its fronds; small plantlets develop on the tops of the mature leaves and these can be cut off and potted.

The most commonly grown *Asplenium* is the bird's nest fern, *A. nidus,* which comes from tropical Australia, and from parts of tropical Asia such as southern Japan. This fern lives high up on rainforest trees which is a good way of getting to sunlight. But it's also a tough life because the plant has to cope without soil, with a grave shortage of minerals and no regular water supply.

> **PLANTS** *Asplenium nidus*
> **REGION OF ORIGIN** Tropics
> **WILD HABITAT** Tree-trunks and branches in rainforests
> **HOME HABITAT** Almost anywhere – good for living rooms and offices because of their size
> **COMMON PROBLEMS** Sharply falling temperatures; not enough moisture

Asplenium nidus-avis

The bird's nest fern has evolved an ingenious way round these problems by growing its own compost heap. The base of its large fronds overlap into a big bowl which collects any falling leaves that drop down from the treetops above. The debris rots down into a wet humus and the fern sucks out the goodness using roots which form a dense interwoven mass like a bird's nest – hence its name. So as a house plant, the fern needs very little artificial feeding. The most common failure is through drying out, which causes the fronds to die back and new leaves to buckle. So it needs regular misting, and a damp pebble tray beneath its pot, as well as constantly moist compost. But it shouldn't be allowed to become soggy, especially in winter or the plant will rot.

Living in exposed treetops, the bird's nest fern can also cope with moderate swings in temperature.

The other interesting thing about the bird's nest fern is that it is very long lived, and can survive for 20 – 50 years in the tropics.

In the wild bird's nest ferns receive very strong dappled sunlight, so to grow them as house plants they need good light for strong growth. They do well in reasonably well-lit places, but sunshine in Britain is so weak and short during the winter that growth will suffer unless they are placed in a sunny window or greenhouse, with, ideally, extra light from an artificial grow lamp obtainable from electrical shops.

Astrophytum

See also CACTI

Astrophytum is a star-shaped cactus from Mexico and a very popular house plant. All the astrophytums have curious greyish-white flakes of hair on the surface of the plants. The flowers are large, up to 8 cm (3¼ in) in diameter. Good light is essential and a well-drained compost to prevent waterlogging. Like most cacti, *Astrophytum* must rest over winter when it needs to be kept cool, dry and unwatered. Then the following season it needs a good soaking when the soil dries out, but hardly any other attention. So it is a very easy plant to have in the house, ideal for a dry, warm, sunny living room.

PLANTS *Astrophytum*
REGION OF ORIGIN Mexico
WILD HABITAT Humid shrubland
HOME HABITAT Sunny windowsill
COMMON PROBLEMS Watering during the rest period in winter or humidity in winter causes ugly yellow and brown patches and sometimes rot

---

Azalea, Rhododendron

The manageable indoor varieties of rhododendrons are commonly called azaleas, and are grown for their colourful winter flowers, blooming from November or December to mid-spring. The most popular species, the Indian azalea, is in fact from China and Taiwan, and has the scientific names *Azalea indica* or *Rhododendron simsii*. In Taiwan it comes from cool high temperate forests.

Azalea indica

Rhododendrons in general are often found growing in a similar habitat to heather, in cool mountainous regions. There are even low-growing northern varieties which can survive the extremes of arctic winter. In the home it is important to keep them cool and 10–15°C (50–60°F) is ideal. Warmer temperatures inhibit flowering and cause leaf drop, but they can tolerate temperatures just above freezing.

Because of their natural habitat, azaleas enjoy humid air and a shady position. They should not be allowed to dry out, and need regular soakings. They appreciate a damp pebble tray under their pots. To get them to flower year after year, they need to be potted out in the garden during their rest period, after the azaleas have stopped flowering in April. Lime-free ericaceous compost is needed for repotting and

the best position is a semi-shaded one that catches the cool early morning sun. When the weather turns colder in October they can be brought inside ready to flower in winter, and it is important to bring them in before severe frosts. They can just about stand being placed in a hot, dry, centrally heated living room while they flower, but it isn't the ideal place and the flowers won't last long. A cool hallway without direct sunlight will stop the flowers from developing too fast and keep the plants blooming for longer.

Azalea indica arrived in Europe from China in the early 1800s, and became part of a regular trade in plants known as the 'Eastern Four': azalea, camellia, chrysanthemum and paeonia. They were in constant demand and were brought in, for example, by sailors of the East

PLANTS *Azalea, Rhododendron*
REGION OF ORIGIN China, Taiwan
WILD HABITAT Cool high temperate forests
HOME HABITAT Hallways and cooler rooms such as dining rooms and bedrooms; can be used as a display plant and later moved outdoors
COMMON PROBLEMS Must be kept cool, wet and humid – leaves and buds drop from being kept too warm and dry; incorrect compost used for repotting can cause leaf yellowing and drop

India Company who made some money on the side selling them to rich English gardeners. By the end of the Victorian era hundreds of differently coloured hybrids had been produced: red, white, pink, violet and variegated varieties with two colours in the same flower.

At first keeping azaleas indoors proved very hit and miss, until it was learnt that the roots must be kept cool and well watered to give a good head of flowers. The Victorians found that keeping moss on top of the soil kept the roots cool in summer. They also made a hole in the soil next to the stem to let cool water trickle through to the roots. Another Victorian trick for ensuring a good head of flowers was to expose them to cool evening temperatures, 5°C – 10°C (40 – 50°F), and in the summer they would get a train of plants to flower by bringing them up one after another from a cold cellar.

Barrel cactus
See *Ferocactus*

Begonia

Begonias are an enormous group of plants widespread throughout the tropics, from habitats ranging from tropical rainforests in Amazonia and West Africa to cool forests in the Andes and Himalayas.

They are grown for their multicoloured leaves or flowers or both, but botanists have classified the thousand or more species of begonia into three types based on their root systems: tubers, rhizomes and fibrous roots.

The rhizome begonias tend to come from hardier climates and they can survive periods of drought by storing water and food in their rhizomes. The rhizomes also 'scramble' over the ground and put down roots wherever they touch the soil or moss-covered tree-trunks, and that makes the house plants easy to propagate from rhizome cuttings.

The tuberous begonias are the commonest house plant begonias, and like the rhizome types they can cope with shortages of water by using stored food and water in their tubers.

Fibrous root types are much more delicate and need more watering and feeding.

Begonias will grow in quite shady positions. A north-facing window is good enough for all begonias and east or west aspects are also friendly for fibrous begonias and should have enough light for them to flower as well. But south-facing windows are too bright in summer unless shaded.

A comfortable temperature for humans is good for most begonias, but never place them near central heating radiators or open fires because the hot dry air makes their leaves turn brown and shrivelled at the edges. Also avoid draughts. Only water when the compost in their pots is dry, and give a high potash fertilizer at regular fortnightly intervals while the plant is growing.

Another common feature of begonias is their phenomenal power to propagate from leaf cuttings, which has no apparent relevance to their wild habitat. Leaf cuttings can be lightly scored underneath and laid flat on a good propagating compost. When kept warm at about 21°C (70°F) small plants sprout from the cut part of the leaf. Stem cuttings taken from low down on the parent plant will also grow in similarly warm temperatures.

The name *Begonia* comes from a seventeenth-century Governor of Canada, Michel Begon, who was also a great patron of botany. But it wasn't until 1856 that begonias caught the public's imagination, when *Begonia rex*, one of the first multicoloured foliage plants discovered in India by the Victorians, was introduced to Europe. The beautiful foliage of *B. rex* then became the source of many hybrids and an enormous favourite for Victorian stately homes.

There are now over 10,000 begonia hybrids, including varieties grown for foliage or flowers. Many of the early hybrids were bred by the world-renowned horticulturalists, James Veitch and Son at their London and Exeter nurseries, and by the Lemoines at Nancy in France, but in general the records of those hybridizations are poor and we really are very unsure where many of our modern varieties originated from, which makes growing advice based on their natural history rather patchy.

There is an enormous range of foliage leaf

Left: *Begonia tuberhybrida*
Right: *B. multiflora*

patterns to choose from, such as the iron cross begonia (*Begonia masoniana*) or the dozens of varieties of the stripy-leaved *B. rex*. These begonias are specially adapted to shady tropical forest floors and feature microscopic leaf lenses on their leaf surfaces to scavenge for light. So as house plants they prefer diffuse light away from direct sunlight. They are also susceptible to overwatering and appreciate airy soils without being waterlogged.

Begonia corallina de lucerna

In contrast to *Begonia tuberhybrida*, there are more modest flowering, but hardier, begonias which can be kept all year round. The most common types are called 'cane stemmed begonias' with upright stems and delicate flowers which hang down in bunches. *Begonia corallina de lucerna* is the most popular species and is a cross between a begonia from Malaysia and one from Brazil, grows to about 2 m (6 ft) tall and needs a large pot, about 50 cm (20 in) in diameter. Like all begonias, they don't like strong sunlight but can stand brighter light than most begonias and they are happy in a moderately bright living room. Again, you can tell if the plant is enjoying the light because the leaves are spotty and it flowers all the year round. But in low light it turns greener, darker, thinner and has fewer flowers. *B. corallina de lucerna* also needs humidity and in dry rooms will need to be placed on a wet pebble tray. It also propagates very easily from stem and leaf cuttings and makes a good plant for living rooms.

PLANTS *Begonia corallina de lucerna*
REGION OF ORIGIN Malaysia × Brazil
WILD HABITAT Tropical forest floors open to some sunlight
HOME HABITAT Fairly bright living room, windowsill facing east or west
COMMON PROBLEMS Don't stand close to hot spots such as radiators because the leaves dry out

Begonia rex

Begonia rex comes from the shady forest floors of tropical India. It grows from a rhizome and is easy to propagate from its rhizome and also leaf cuttings. It needs slightly more light than many other begonias, and you can tell if it is happy with the light because dim conditions make the leaves turn darker and the plant stops growing – so it shouldn't be placed at the back of a room. On the other hand, it does not like harsh light next to a window. As for watering, *B. rex* needs lots of air in its soil and is more prone to overwatering than a flowering begonia such as *Begonia corallina de lucerna*. It needs more humidity than many other begonias, but like a lot of the rhizome types, it rests during winter when it hardly needs watering.

PLANTS *Begonia rex*
REGION OF ORIGIN India
WILD HABITAT Shady, humid tropical forest floor
HOME HABITAT Will stand some shade, so good for basement flats and shady rooms
COMMON PROBLEMS It is singed by direct sunlight; needs extra humidity in dry rooms; needs an airy soil mixture

---

Begonia tuberhybrida

The most spectacular large flowering begonias are the tuberous kinds such as *B. tuberhybrida* and its close cousin, *B. tuberhybrida pendula*, which makes a beautiful hanging basket display. These begonias originally came from the Andes where they grew in moist crevices in rocky outcrops on patchy soil rich in guano. So as house plants they appreciate a light airy soil rich in phosphates. Their ancestors also grew in the shelter of hilltop boulders where low dense fog hung over the coastal hills, and that makes humidity for the house plants important as well.

But although these begonias have lovely large blooms they are very difficult to keep in flower for long and are fussy about their watering and

---

PLANTS *Begonia tuberhybrida*
REGION OF ORIGIN Andes
WILD HABITAT Rock crevices in foggy hills
HOME HABITAT Cool, semi-shaded positions or east- or west-facing windowsills
COMMON PROBLEMS Difficult to keep flowering, mustn't be overwatered or have too much light; only water when the compost in the pot is dry and give a high potash fertilizer at intervals while the plant is growing

---

light. So, reluctantly, they are best treated as temporary house plants which can be thrown out after flowering.

Blushing bromeliad
See *Neoregelia*

BROMELIADS

High up in the canopies of tropical forests are plants clinging on for dear life. They are called bromeliads from the sub-tropical and tropical Americas and they live a tightrope sort of life, grasping hold of trees with their roots, completely out of touch with the ground below. This is a precarious lifestyle because they have to endure long periods without rainwater, scorched under the intense tropical sun, no soil to feed on and the problem of staying firmly anchored to tree bark during winds and storms. Yet it's worth all these risks because the bromeliads reach sunlight without having to go to the trouble of growing tall stems like trees. You could say that they are cheating, because they're riding piggyback on the trees, and give the trees nothing back in return. And it obviously pays off, because bromeliads are extremely common in the tropical forests of Latin America.

In the home most bromeliads do better attached to moss poles or mock tree stumps, mimicking their wild situation. To do this you take them out of their pot and wind the stems with a 'bandage' of moss or fibrous coir tied

together with nylon fishing line. The whole bundle is then attached at an angle of about 45° to the pole, using more nylon thread, or plastic-coated wire for large plants. The exception is for the pineapple which is a ground-dwelling bromeliad and should be left in its pot. The other exception is the air plants (tillandsias) which can be stuck to pieces of log or bark with a mastic glue, but you have to be careful not to glue their leaf bases which have tiny roots. You might wonder what gluing air plants like this has to do with their life in the wild, but they grow naturally from seeds which wedge themselves in cracks in the tree bark.

Bromeliads have evolved some ingenious ways of getting their water and minerals. Many have their very own water tanks made from leaves tightly clasped together into cups, some of them holding up to 5 litres (just over a gallon) of water. High up in the trees these small ponds of water are sheer luxury for animals in need of a drink, but frogs and other water creatures actually live in them like an aquarium. Not that it does the plant any harm, because the wastes from the animals help feed the plant with the minerals it desperately needs.

Bromeliads have other ways of feeding. As rain-water cascades down a tree it leaches out minerals which the bromeliads absorb. The plants' roots also ferret out juicy morsels of rotting debris trapped in the nooks and crannies in the tree's bark.

Sometimes bromeliads feed off ant nests perched on the trees. The rotting organic debris collected by the ants makes a fertile patch of humus for the bromeliad to grow on. The ants appear to like the arrangement because in many cases they actually sow the plant seeds in their nests in the first place. Many ants nest among the roots of bromeliads and may actually gather dead leaves, seeds and debris of all kinds, and may play a vital role in providing soil for the plant. So one way and another the bromeliad scratches out an intriguing existence under very demanding circumstances.

Bromeliads have another trick up their leaves for coping with drought and harsh light. The leaves are covered in minute umbrella-like hairs which give the leaf a grey-green colour. The hairs protect the stomata (leaf pores) and this helps cut down water losses during drought. They also help block the intense ultraviolet rays of the sun.

Certain bromeliads such as *Neoregelia* 'blush' when they flower. The centre of the almost green leaf rosette flushes red when the flowers appear in the centre and this probably helps advertise the flowers to insect or bird pollinators.

Bromeliads are now becoming more popular because of their big showy leaves and bright flowers. Being tropical, they need warmth (with a minimum of about 10°C, 50°F) as well as

Left: *Aechmea fasciata*
Right: *A. recurrata*

LEFT Adapted to living in hot, dry treetops in the tropics, these air plants survive much hardship.

Bromeliads live a bizarre life, perched in trees without ever touching the ground. Their leaf rosettes collect rainwater and the roots search out rotting debris.

light, plenty of moisture (by misting with a spray), and because their roots tend to be small they only need watering when their compost dries out. They often need a support to lean on. Because they grow in the wild on small patches of humus and moss, they need a peat-based or peat-like compost.

As we have discussed earlier, the most natural way to grow bromeliads is on a 'tree' of bark, and because the plants grow at an angle, just like the bromeliad colonies in the wild, they are more likely to be watered properly. Overfilling the vases or cups can cause rot, particularly in the home where temperatures are cool. But if

bromeliads are grown in pots, then after watering their leaf cups they should ideally be tilted at an angle of 45° over the sink to drain off the surplus water.

BROMELIADS included in this book:

Aechmea	*Neoregelia*
Ananas comosus (pineapple)	*Tillandsia*
	Vriesea
Guzmania	

Busy Lizzie

[*Impatiens wallerana*]

Busy Lizzie first became known to the west through John Kirk, the physician and naturalist who accompanied Livingstone in the 1850s. He found it in Zanzibar, but in fact *Impatiens wallerana* grows throughout Tanzania and Mozambique. Today's house plants are all hybrids from East Africa and more recently from those species collected from New Guinea in the early 1970s, and none of the wild species are common in the home.

Busy Lizzies grow in rainforest clearings, on fallen tree stumps and living trees and on damp mossy banks. They prefer these slightly exposed locations and so in the home the plants need bright light, but not hot direct summer sun. In this strong light they will flower profusely but need plenty of water during the growing season.

The flowers of *Impatiens wallerana* are pollinated by butterflies with the large flat petals acting as 'landing pads'. Other members of the *Impatiens* genus have differently shaped petals designed for bee and other insect pollinators.

PLANTS *Impatiens wallerana*
REGION OF ORIGIN Tanzania, Mozambique
WILD HABITAT In rainforest clearings growing in spreading clumps along the ground or on mossy tree bark
HOME HABITAT Bright location in living room
COMMON PROBLEMS Underwatering makes them wilt fast; lack of flowering often due to too little light

Hybrids of *Impatiens* have been bred to produce almost continuous flowers on short stems and there are a great number of different colours available. The New Guinea hybrids from species such as *Impatiens hawkeri* are also rainforest plants but have longer leaves than the African varieties and the leaves are often of two colours.

Busy Lizzies are easy to grow but need to be watered frequently in the summer, when they can start wilting the day after being watered. They are not particularly temperature sensitive but 10–13°C (50–55°F) is the minimum. Stem

Impatiens wallerana 'Sultanii'

cuttings which root easily all the year round are the best way to propagate new plants.

Between the teeth of the leaf margins of *Impatiens* are small nodules which pump out water. They are activated when the humidity is so intense that simple evaporation from the leaf pores (stomata) no longer works well. This is particularly important in the humid tropics.

Butterworts

[*Pinguicula*]

See also CARNIVOROUS PLANTS

Butterworts are rather simple carnivorous traps, relying on tiny sticky hairs on their leaves to glue down small insects such as midges and gnats. They grow worldwide in boggy, marshy wetlands where the acid water and lack of nourishment is supplemented by carnivorousness.

Like all carnivorous plants, they mustn't be left to dry out or given hard tap-water. They need a constant supply of rain-water or distilled water or the water from a defrosted fridge. They are also particularly sensitive to fluorine treatment in tap-water, which can give the effect of burnt leaves.

To help recreate the bogland conditions it originally came from, the butterwort's pot can be stood in a shallow saucer of water. It also does very well in a terrarium where the moisture is constant, but the lid should allow for some ventilation as excessive moisture will cause rot. Another tip for the terrarium is to

use a peat and sphagnum moss mix or live sphagnum moss mixed with chips of bark or coir.

Butterworts come from temperate areas, or the cooler regions of the sub-tropics, so they are used to living in seasons: in summer they like to be kept warm and in the winter to be cool, although not lower than 5°C (41°F) as most are not frost-hardy. New plants can be grown in the spring from seeds.

Most of the butterworts enjoy the sun, but the Mexican butterwort (*Pinguicula moranensis*) dislikes being in full sun for too long. There are several species of butterwort which are good for keeping as house plants including *Pinguicula vulgaris*, 15 cm (6 in) tall, from the temperate northern hemisphere, and *Pinguicula grandiflora*, 20 cm (8 in) tall, from western and northern Europe.

Like all carnivorous plants, butterworts do not need fertilizer or even dead meat, and it's best to let them catch their own living prey, such as midges and other small flies.

The name *Pinguicula* comes from the Latin *pinguis* meaning fat, and refers to their thick greasy leaves. Apart from being attractive to look at, the leaves were also used by Laplanders for making cheese, thanks to the digestive enzymes in the leaf glands.

CACTI

Cacti are to the plant kingdom what camels are to animals – the supreme drought-tolerators. But how are they adapted to dry conditions?

Cacti do their utmost to stop losing water. They are thick-skinned, leafless stems, full of thick juice which holds water, and with pores in the stem that open in the cool of night instead of during the day as is the situation with most plants. The leaves have been turned into spines

---

PLANTS *Pinguicula*
REGIONS OF ORIGIN Almost worldwide, from temperate to sub-tropical
WILD HABITAT Sunny positions
HOME HABITAT Bright windowsill in ventilated terrarium
COMMON PROBLEMS They need acid or neutral water instead of tap-water, which can cause blackening and brown chemical burns

---

Bring a touch of desert to a sunny windowsill. Cacti are robust house plants provided they're watered in summer and cool and dry in winter.

for defending the plant from animals and catching dew. And because conventional leaves have been dispensed with, the stem is green and does the photosynthesis.

Given their spartan lifestyle, it's hardly surprising that cacti are slow-growing plants, especially during droughts. But this is only true up to a point – as soon as it rains they are supremely well adapted for growing rapidly. Their root buds burst into life, growing extensive networks of fibrous roots which absorb huge amounts of water. Some cacti grow wide networks of surface roots to take advantage of water running over the ground, even though the rains only last a short time. This way they absorb huge quantities of water – the saguaro cacti can weigh up to a ton when full of water (in fact, they become something of a hazard during thunder-storms because lightning often hits them, turning their water to steam and making the cacti explode like a bomb!). But it's a myth that all cacti can stand intense heat. Many cacti such as *Gymnocalycium* and *Neoporteria* grow next to boulders where it is cooler and more water is held underground. There is also a thought that the spines on the stem could help condense mist or dew – some cacti grow in misty regions and their spines are covered in a special lichen which absorbs moisture from the air like blotting paper. This is probably why in cultivation cacti respond well to mist sprays during the early morning or evening in summer.

However, the golden rule (which applies to the northern hemisphere) is not to water them during any month with the letter 'r' in it, e.g., during the winter months. This is their resting period when their growth stops and they go into a plant-equivalent of hibernation – if they are watered during this period they may rot, or

Cacti are camels of the plant world! Tough skins help keep the stems full of water to survive long droughts.

CACTI included in this book:

Astrophytum	*Ferocactus*
Christmas and Easter	*Gymnocalycium*
cacti (*Zygocactus*	*Mammillaria*
Rhipsalidopsis)	

grow straggly, or fail to flower the following season. It is also very important to give the cacti sun in the winter because that also encourages flowering the next year as it ripens the plant. However, because cacti often have to tolerate cold nights in the desert they can be kept quite cool during the winter, 7–10°C (45–50°F), and some will even survive freezing temperatures, but be careful not to keep them humid because it makes them rot.

Then the following spring, water them lightly, and slowly increase the watering into the summer and they will flower well in May, June, early July. During the summer cacti also need plenty of sunshine because they are adapted to bright strong desert sunshine. Some have waxy blooms or hairs covering their stems to cut down sunlight and heat.

Cacti grow in poor rocky or sandy soils so it is important to get their compost right – plenty of grit with very little peat, which should never be waterlogged and never stood on water. Yet despite their poor soil in the wild they respond surprisingly well to fertilizer once a month during the growing season.

Cacti can be grown surprisingly easily from seed. If the seeds are germinated in plastic bags to keep the humidity high they sprout in two to three days in warm temperatures – an airing cupboard at 16–21°C (60–70°F) is ideal. In two to three months the seedlings can be planted out in boxes. This technique has revolutionized cacti culture over the past 25 years, and helped take some of the pressure off the wild populations being illegally plundered by collectors. But unfortunately collectors are still digging up wild plants even though they often do not grow well in cultivation.

They do well on sunny windowsills, and appreciate being turned round regularly to sun them all over. Because they come from dry climates they do not need humidity but they do need watering especially in summer when they are growing and when their soil is dry, never wet.

Caladium

[Angel's wings]

See also AROIDS

These are beautiful plants from the forest clearings of tropical America and the West Indies, grown for their large delicate coloured leaves. The leaves are easily damaged by dry air or rough handling and need plenty of humidity. The Victorians got round this problem by growing them in glass boxes called Wardian cases, the precursors of the modern terrarium. But nowadays there are hardier hybrids which survive in less humidity, a warm location not less than about 12°C (54°F) in the house, although away from direct sunlight. They still need humidity, but an alternative to keeping them in glass tanks is standing them on a tray of moist pebbles and misting them regularly. And they are worth the trouble because of their beautifully coloured arrow shaped leaves. *Caladium humboldtii* is one of the original species collected from the rainforests of Brazil and the hybrids such as 'angel's wings' are collectively known as 'Hortulanum' hybrids with stunning multicoloured foliage.

PLANTS *Caladium*
REGION OF ORIGIN Tropical Americas and West Indies
WILD HABITAT Forest clearings
HOME HABITAT Humid shady places such as kitchens
COMMON PROBLEMS Light watering during the rest period, otherwise the plant can rot or grow spindly

Calathea makoyana

The caladiums have a long resting period in the autumn and winter when their leaves die off. But the plants don't have to be thrown away because they have a thick tuberous root which stores enough food to regrow the following season, helped by warm conditions. Occasionally they bloom with inconspicuous spathe-like inflorescences typical of aroids.

Calathea

These are very popular foliage plants from tropical forest floors of Latin America and West Indies. They all have magnificent leaf patterns, varying from fishbone patterns to blotches, and their size ranges from compact, rounded clumps to large specimens several feet high. Because

PLANTS *Calathea*
REGION OF ORIGIN Tropical Americas, West Indies
WILD HABITAT Rainforest floor
HOME HABITAT Kitchens are good for humidity in a semi-shade position away from direct midday sun
COMMON PROBLEMS Dry air causes poor growth and brown leaf tips

they come from the floor of tropical forests they are used to thriving in warm, constant temperatures, about 15–20°C (60–70°F), high humidity and varying amounts of shade. The warmth is fairly easy to supply in a heated home; the shade is best given by standing just away from windows or letting them get early morning or evening sunlight and avoiding the midday sun. But the humidity is more difficult in a home, and dry air results in poor growth and brown tips to the leaves. So, particularly in a living room, they need extra help with humidity: by standing the pots on wet trays of pebbles; putting out saucers of open water under the leaves; or misting the leaves. They need watering well in spring and summer when they are growing, but waterlogging, or alternatively, drying out the soil damages the leaves.

Some calatheas have superbly coloured leaf veins. One species, *Calathea ornata*, has a deep bronzy leaf on which the veins look as if they have been painted light pink, and these leaf-vein patterns might attract insects to pollinate the rather dull-looking flowers.

Other calatheas have a dark and light green fishbone pattern, and there's some thought that this may be a camouflage. Seen from an animal's point of view, the leaf looks like it has already been chewed up by another animal, putting them off eating it themselves. It's an intriguing theory, and you can see for yourself how dramatic the leaf patterns are by shining a light behind the leaf.

Many *Calathea* species have leaves which move. Species growing in semi-shade swivel their leaves round during the day to follow the sun in order to fuel their photosynthesis. But plants growing in more exposed areas protect themselves from being scorched by the harsh midday sun by folding up towards noon and then folding down again towards dusk. This is why calatheas are sometimes known as prayer plants, a name reserved here for the marantas.

Callisia

There are about twelve species of *Callisia* which come from tropical America. The most popular house plant *Callisia elegans* (previously called *Setcreasea striata*) comes from the moist mountain area of central Mexico around cities such as Oaxaca. It is low growing and forms huge patches of ground cover on rocky soil. *Callisia* is a close relative of *Tradescantia* (spiderwort) but it has longer stems and the upper surface of the leaves is a deep matt green with bold white stripes. The undersides of the leaves are purple, and if you are lucky you might see the small creamy flowers which only last for about a day.

Callisia thrives in averagely warm living rooms, but even though it is a mountainous plant it will not tolerate temperatures below 5°C (41°F). Like others of its *Tradescantia* relatives, the main thing for keeping *Callisia* healthy is lots of bright light. It needs watering throughout the spring, summer and autumn but less so in winter when its growth slows down. It is very easy to propagate from stem cuttings taken in the growing seasons.

This is a great trailing plant for hanging baskets and overflowing pots.

PLANTS *Callisia*
REGION OF ORIGIN Tropical Latin America
WILD HABITAT Rocky soils
HOME HABITAT Bright windowsill in kitchen
COMMON PROBLEMS Lack of water

CARNIVOROUS PLANTS

To understand how to grow carnivorous plants you need to know something about their home backgrounds. They tend to live in boggy marshes with acid water, where nutrients are in poor supply and few other plants can survive. The carnivorous plants have evolved meat-eating to overcome this spartan life. Their leaves have taken over from roots in feeding, and their roots are reduced to short stubby things used for anchorage and absorbing water.

Carnivorous plants have a terrible reputation for being difficult to look after, but much of their notoriety is undeserved. Here are a few tips and a few myths.

1 You do not need to keep all carnivorous plants in heated greenhouses because many of them are not tropical. The ones listed here are temperate or at most sub-tropical and some can even take freezing conditions.
2 You should not feed them meat because they are designed to catch their own food and they usually need living animals.
3 In the wild, carnivorous plants tend to grow in acid, boggy waters, so they will need acid or neutral water, such as distilled or rain-water; tap-water is often fatal because it is usually alkaline.
4 The plants must never be allowed to dry out because they tend to come from boglands.
5 Carnivorous plants also have special soil needs because of their bogland origins but there is a variety of soils to choose from, usually based on a peat-sand mixture. However, there is a certain irony in using this because the digging up of peat for horticulture has ruined many of the bogs that carnivorous plants come from. So a more ecologically sound alternative is to use live sphagnum moss mixed in with chips of bark, or coir.
6 Carnivorous plants genuinely need animals to feed on – they don't kill them for some sort of sadistic kick. Once the animal has been killed, its digested remains are used for the

plant's own growth and development, and without a carnivorous diet they become stunted.

Because the carnivorous plants included here come from temperate or sub-tropical areas, they tend to have seasonal growth. They start growing well in spring, reach full fitness around May to August, then slowly turn stunted in autumn and stop growing altogether during winter, when the plants can look so dead many people mistakenly throw them out. Because the plants tell what season it is from the hours of daylight each day, you can fool them into growing throughout winter by using artificial lights, such as special plant grow lamps available from garden or electrical shops, or using ordinary domestic fluorescent tubes hung close to the plants.

Many of the plants included here are also becoming endangered through illegal picking for the plant trade.

> CARNIVOROUS PLANTS included in this book:
>
> Butterworts *Darlingtonia* *Sarracenia*
> Sundew Venus flytrap

Ceropegia
[Rosary plant, string of hearts]

Ceropegia is a succulent plant from warm temperate savanna and forests in Natal, South Africa, and Zimbabwe, and this fairly rugged environment makes it a fairly easy house plant to grow. Its trailing stems grow from a woody tuber and meander through and over surrounding plants and small shrubs, rooting at intervals where they find earth. This trailing habit makes them good plants for hanging baskets or on a shelf near a south-facing window or from the windowsills themselves, matching their hanging growth from shrubs or rocks in their natural habitat.

The way the stems root regularly into small plantlets makes *Ceropegia* good for propagating. Take stem cuttings complete with a piece of baby tuber attached so they can take root.

Ceropegia does not experience frost in its natural habitat so it needs to be kept above 8–10°C (46–50°F). During its growing season the plant is happiest with only a little water which helps to make its leaves fat and well coloured; too much water turns the leaves thin and pale. Thanks to its tough origins, the plant enjoys sun or shade, and can stand the dry air of a living room.

The tiny *Ceropegia* flowers appear in late

PLANTS   *Ceropegia woodii*
REGION OF ORIGIN   Natal in South Africa, and Zimbabwe
WILD HABITAT   Temperate savanna and forests
HOME HABITAT   Bright rooms, such as living rooms
COMMON PROBLEMS   Overwatering which turns the leaves thin and pale

Ceropegia woodii

summer and look like elaborate Edwardian lampshades, lacy frills and all. The top of the flower is black and olive and forms a frilly lid below which are openings with scent-attractive areas. Inside the flowers there is a slippery one-way chute down into a translucent light purple prison below, which features intriguing 'windows' around the sexual organs. The bewildered insects batter around this area, where they find some nectar and become covered in pollen. But they have to wait, sometimes for several days, until the hairs inside the flower wither and the flower tilts horizontally and lets them escape.

Chamaedorea elegans

See Parlour palm

Chlorophytum comosum

See Spider plant

Christmas and Easter cacti

[*Zygocactus, Rhipsalidopsis*]

See also CACTI

These are true cacti but they are very different from the desert ones. They live as epiphytes, perched on trees in the dense tropical rainforests of the Amazon, and like other rainforest plants they need warmth, moist air, and diffuse light – a far cry from their desert cousins. They have what look like stubby leaves, but are in fact flattened segmented stems.

In their Brazilian home both the Christmas and Easter cacti hang down from the branches of trees, growing in small pockets of humus caught in the cracks of the tree bark. But they can also grow on steep, shaded rock faces, where the segmented stems sometimes break off to form a colony of new plants below the bushy parent plant. This makes the house plants easy to propagate from the stem segments. Cuttings can be taken in the summer, using the segment at the tip of the flattened stems, left to dry for a few days and rooted in soil.

In the wild, they get bright dappled light beneath the upper layers of the forest canopy, and of course they get far more rain-water and humidity than desert cacti. They absorb this moisture using aerial roots which dangle in the air. So in a dry home, a damp pebble tray beneath the pot is a very good idea.

To reproduce the thin, naturally airy soil a mixture of about two-thirds peat or coir to one-third vermiculite is ideal. When they are growing, they need to be watered regularly and fed with a liquid fertilizer every fortnight. The plants can be repotted annually but they flower best when less than about three years old.

Temperatures in their wild habitat are on average about 15–18°C (59–65°F), although surprisingly for a jungle plant they can tolerate temperatures as low as 5°C (40°F).

The species most commonly called Christmas cacti are *Zygocactus truncata* and

Zygocactus buckleyi, the latter of which is a hybrid of *Zygocactus truncata* and *Zygocactus russelliana*. There are several types (cultivars) of the hybrid *Zygocactus buckleyi*, too, such as the purple and red flowering 'Noris', or 'Weinachtsfreude' which has mottled red flowers with a purple centre. As usual, botanists can't make their minds up about naming the plants, and the genus *Zygocactus* is equally well known as *Schlumbergera*, which would have pleased Frederick Schlumberger the nineteenth-century Belgian botanist after whom they were named. The Easter cactus is the very closely related *Rhipsalidopsis gaertneri* and, confusingly, is also called *Schlumbergera gaertneri*.

Out of flower you can tell the Christmas and Easter cacti apart because the Christmas cactus has toothed edges to its flattened stems, but in the Easter cactus these are smooth and rounded. Of course it is the flowering time that is the main point of distinction, with the Christmas cactus flowering during the short days of the year, around Christmas time, and the Easter cactus in the longer days of spring.

It is not difficult to get both the Christmas and Easter cacti to flower year after year – the trick is to give them rest periods. They need a period when they are kept cool and sparsely watered, although the soil should never dry out. The Easter cactus has its dry rest period from late September until the flower buds start to form in mid-March, when watering is stepped up. In contrast, the Christmas cactus has two rest periods, the first in February and March, shortly after flowering, and the second from late September to mid November when again watering is increased as the flower buds begin to grow. Both types really benefit from being left outdoors in a shaded spot from June to August, but they can become exotic food for slugs if you aren't careful!

One interesting facet of flowering in the forest cacti is that the buds bend themselves towards light. But once the buds have formed, you shouldn't change the orientation of the plants because the flower buds will try to

PLANTS Christmas cactus, Easter cactus (*Zygocactus* (*Schlumbergera*), *Rhipsalidopsis*)
REGION OF ORIGIN Brazil
WILD HABITAT Tree branches or rocky slopes in rainforests
HOME HABITAT Warm, humid and indirect light, good for kitchens and bathrooms
COMMON PROBLEMS Must have a rest period without watering to stimulate flowering the following season

realign themselves and fall off. You can take the plant away for watering if necessary, but you have to remember which way it was facing when you put it back.

Finally, it is amazing that cacti grow in both deserts and jungles. In evolution, cacti probably started life in jungles, then adapted to arid lands, and finally re-entered the primeval forests, and so have retained a lot of the cacti features. But this is only theory.

Chinese fig
See *Ficus pumila*

Chrysalidocarpus
[Butterfly palm, swift death]

This is a group of feathery palms. There are just over 20 species in the wild, 18 from Madagascar, two in the Comoro Islands and a species in Pemba Island. They have cane-like stems although there is one wild species, *Chrysalidocarpus decipiens* which is a bottle-shaped palm, having a swollen base to its stem. They are mostly species living in relatively shaded habitats in forest undergrowth.

The one species that is an outstanding house plant is *Chrysalidocarpus lutescens*, the butterfly palm (also called *Areca lutescens*). The leaflets are twisted in a beautiful pattern, and it was once the most popular indoor palm before the Kentia parlour palms were introduced.

Chrysalidocarpus lutescens

PLANTS *Chrysalidocarpus*
REGION OF ORIGIN Madagascar
WILD HABITAT Growing in clumps in shaded undergrowth
HOME HABITAT Partially shaded; should stand on damp pebble tray in warm rooms; large specimens are good for a conservatory
COMMON PROBLEMS Repotting retards growth; waterlogging and sudden cold can kill; nutritional imbalance – give a liquid feed fortnightly in the summer

---

In the wild the butterfly palm forms clumps growing in a warm and humid climate. It needs constant generous watering when it is hot, but only needs a little moisture in the winter. *Chrysalidocarpus* is sometimes classified as an 'eighty eighty' palm, meaning that it enjoys 80 per cent humidity and 80°F (26°C) which is an ideal greenhouse climate but would lead to serious rot in the home. Under these ideal conditions it can reach the ceiling but it can survive cooled conditions down to 10°C (50°F) although growth is slower. Its seeds are difficult to grow at temperatures below 25°C (77°F).

Chrysalidocarpus can be propagated by

offshoots: cut them and give them a pot of their own when they are about 15 cm (6 in) high. They need a well-drained soil with terracotta crocking at the bottom of the pot as waterlogged palms can die. Potentially, in a large container, this palm could grow well over 3 m (9 ft) tall with fronds 1 m (3 ft) long, but if it is kept in a relatively small pot, about 30 cm (12 in) in diameter, it will remain a manageable size. Once you have decided on the size of pot it is best to stick with it, because like all palms the butterfly palms hate being repotted: it stunts their growth at best and kills them at worst. The butterfly palm is certainly a challenging house plant, but you shouldn't let the alarming trade nickname for *Chrysalidocarpus*, 'swift death', put you off because they are beautiful plants.

The name *Chrysalidocarpus* is probably derived from chrysalid, the golden butterfly pupae, and *karpos*, the Greek for fruit, which describes the seeds of some species.

Chrysanthemum

The original *Chrysanthemum* species bear little relation to the modern house plants which have been bred and hybridized for thousands of years.

They probably came from China, and were perennials so they could survive frost in winter with underground storage organs, and were strictly autumn or summer flowering. But now breeding, artificial light and chemical treatments have tricked the plants into flowering all the year round. *Chrysanthemum* is one of the most popular house plants and is

now one of the most highly bred and treated.

Chrysanthemums need good light but should be kept out of direct sunlight. They need good watering, but they don't mind dry air. They are usually sold coming into flower but the most important thing for long flowering is to keep them in cool places, ideally between 6–16°C (43–61°F), and then they may flower for over two months.

It is impossible to keep chrysanthemums indoors as dwarf flowering plants in their second year – if you don't want to throw them out or keep them outdoors as tall plants. They can be replanted after flowering but the success rate isn't high.

Cobra lily

See *Darlingtonia*

Codiaeum

[Croton]

Crotons originate from the shrub layer of hot and humid forests in Malaysia, Indonesia and the Pacific islands. In the wild they grow up into bushes and small trees but in pots they stay as bushes with stunningly coloured leaves.

They appreciate good light as this helps the colouring in their leaves, but they don't like being stood in direct bright sunlight. They enjoy a windowsill without the midday sun, provided they don't have cold draughts or other big swings in temperature. Ideally they like a fairly constant 16°–20°C (60°–68°F) as they

---

PLANTS *Chrysanthemum*
REGION OF ORIGIN China
WILD HABITAT Cool hillsides
HOME HABITAT Good light in any room, temporary display
COMMON PROBLEMS Too much warmth shortens the life of the flowers

---

PLANTS *Codiaeum*
REGION OF ORIGIN South-east Asia and Polynesia
WILD HABITAT Shrub layer of hot, humid forests
HOME HABITAT Kitchen windowsills
COMMON PROBLEMS Cold draughts, dry air leading to plagues of pests and leaves dropping

would experience in their natural tropical forests.

Having so much foliage they also need plenty of watering, but the roots can rot if they are stood in water. Coming from a humid climate, they also need to be kept humid by standing on wet pebble trays and sprayed in warm rooms. Dry air causes all sorts of problems: the leaves can drop off and infestations of scale insects, mealy bug, and red spider mites can attack. Mealy bug, which look like cotton wool, and scale insects which look like small brown/white discs can be removed by dabbing them with a cotton-bud soaked in methylated spirit. The spider mites, which cause a dustiness on the leaf's underside and a yellow streaking all over, will be curbed just by constant misting with water underneath the leaves to stop the mites breeding. However, if you are feeling in an apocalyptic mood you can use a chemical spray such as malathion.

Cordyline

Cordyline species cover a great range of distribution, from New Zealand to eastern Asia, and the two main kinds available need quite different conditions.

Cordyline australis (syn. *Dracaena indivisa*), the cabbage palm, comes from New Zealand and grows at high altitude, so it can tolerate great swings in temperature or coolness which makes it a good strong house plant, although it is also used to bright conditions. This makes it ideal in a large unheated room or porch, but it

---

PLANTS *Cordyline australis* (*Dracaena indivisa*)
REGION OF ORIGIN New Zealand
WILD HABITAT Mountainous shrubs
HOME HABITAT Cool and bright hallways; gives tropical look to chilly rooms
COMMON PROBLEMS Dry and very hot conditions will produce brown edges on the leaves; in extreme cases overwatering can kill in winter, but it is not a difficult plant to keep

---

PLANTS *Cordyline terminalis* (*Dracaena terminalis*)
REGION OF ORIGIN South-east Asia
WILD HABITAT Shrubs and trees of sub-tropical or tropical forests
HOME HABITAT Well-lit, humid positions, such as kitchens
COMMON PROBLEM Dry air makes the leaf tips turn brown

---

needs a lot of space because it grows like a shrub and reaches a large size, up to 2 m (6 ft) tall. Although they are almost frost-hardy – and can even grow outside in places like Torquay in south-west England – they should ideally be kept above about 10°C (50°F). *Cordyline australis* needs to be watered in summer but just kept moist in winter, and as it is a slow-growing species it should only need repotting every other year. A good plant for a cool office.

In contrast, *Cordyline terminalis* (syn. *Dracaena terminalis*), the ti plant, is tropical and can tolerate some shade. Polynesians grow

---

Cordyline glauca

it around their houses for luck which is why it is also called the goodluck plant. Being tropical, the plants do not like big fluctuations in temperature and prefer warmth, about 13°–20°C (55–68°F) – lower temperatures stop the plant growing. They also need plenty of watering and if kept too dry they go into a rest period. Coming from a humid natural atmosphere they also need misting as they suffer from brown leaf tips in dry air.

This plant also has an interesting way of propagation because it has 'toes' on its roots, and if you cut them off and plant them in standard potting mixture they will grow into new plants.

Creeping fig

See *Ficus pumila*

Crocus

These bulbs come from the mountainous areas of eastern Mediterranean countries, the Middle East and Asia. The house plant crocuses are usually large hybrids of the wild species, a process of hybridization that began over five hundred years ago in Turkey when collections of bulb plants were highly prized in the gardens of the Ottoman Turks and Mughal princes.

Most of the indoor varieties flower in early spring, but there are also autumn-flowering crocuses that can be grown. In the wild, the spring flowering crocuses survive in extremely tough conditions, such as those found on Turkish mountainsides, almost all the year round. The summers are hot and dry, and the winters freezing cold, so the crocuses have to fit their flowering season into the short springtime. The flower buds develop under the snow, ready to shoot up as soon as the spring thaw starts. Once they have opened, the flowers attract early flying insects to pollinate them, seed is set and the plant dies back into its underground corm and survives the long hot dry summer.

The autumn-flowering crocuses grow on the Caucasus mountains, the steppes of central Mongolia and in northern Greece. These plants make use of the cooler autumn conditions and begin to flower in October. The autumn-flowering crocuses flower first and then grow their leaves, a curious piece of timing, maybe geared to attracting available pollinating insects.

Bearing in mind their natural seasons, spring crocuses need a dry rest over summer and a cool winter and springtime. The best way to keep potted crocuses is to plant them out in their pots during autumn, then bring them into a cool room in the house when they have begun to flower in early spring. A good potting soil can be made from a mixture of sand and John Innes No 2 compost. The corms need to be pushed down into the soil to a depth of about twice their circumference.

There are endless suitable hybrids for indoor potting, such as *Crocus chrysanthus* 'Cream Beauty' or the later flowering *Crocus vernus* 'Joan of Arc' (white), 'Victor Hugo' (glossy purple), and 'Yellow Mammoth'. Alternatively, autumn flowering can be achieved with bulbs of species such as *Crocus speciosus* with hybrids such as 'Alba' and 'Oxonian'.

Different types of crocus are found at various altitudes, and come into flower at different times, probably because of the gradient in temperature up the mountain. In south-west Turkey the wild white species, *Crocus fleisheri* grows at about 1000 m (3000 ft), low to the ground in open sunny grassed areas and sheltered by occasional slabs of rock. Just 300 m (985 ft) further up the mountain, the yellow species, such as *Crocus flavus*, predominate and come into flower later.

PLANTS *Crocus*
REGION OF ORIGIN Eastern Mediterranean, Middle East, Asia
WILD HABITAT Mountains
HOME HABITAT Cool rooms
COMMON PROBLEM Too much warmth makes the flower die

LEFT Autumn crocuses originate from the eastern Mediterranean where their corms keep them safe during the long summer drought and provide food for the winter and spring.

Some of the wild crocuses are extremely rare and threatened by collectors. For example, the light blue *Crocus baytopiorum* is only known from seven sites in Turkey and was only described in the mid-1970s, so it has not been around long enough to hybridize as a house plant. On the specialist market such bulbs sell for £3 or £4 each in Britain. The British organization FFPS (Flora and Fauna Preservation Society) is working with the Turkish society for Nature Conservation (known as DHKD) to find sustainable ways of propagating such bulbs.

The name crocus comes from the Greek word for saffron, *krokos*, a highly expensive yellow dye which comes from the reproductive part of the Greek crocus *Crocus sativus*. It takes a quarter of a million hand-picked crocuses to produce just a pound of saffron.

Croton
See *Codiaeum*

Ctenanthe

Ctenanthe comes from the same family as *Maranta* and *Calathea*. It grows at ground level in the hot, humid jungles of Brazil. Like *Maranta* and *Calathea* it, too, is grown for its stunning variegated foliage which is mottled with darker green, cream or pink, with green or purple undersides.

PLANTS *Ctenanthe*
REGION OF ORIGIN Brazil
WILD HABITAT Tropical rainforests
HOME HABITAT Humid rooms such as bathrooms and kitchens or living rooms if kept humid enough
COMMON PROBLEMS Not enough humidity turns the leaves brown

Ctenanthe lubbersiana

Much of the domestic life of *Ctenanthe* reflects its way of life in the jungle. It can tolerate shade, but needs good light to keep its leaf markings, although it does not like direct sunlight or temperatures under about 15°C (60°F). It is important to create good humidity by regularly misting with tepid water and also to water with tepid water when the top of the soil starts to dry out. But don't let the roots stand in water and give the pots good drainage, otherwise the roots can rot.

Cyathea
See Tree ferns

Cyclamen

Cyclamens come from Mediterranean climates, with mountainous and coastal species growing on rocky soils. There are about 20 species in all, and most wild kinds are spring flowering, but there are also some autumn-flowering species.

PLANTS *Cyclamen persicum*
REGION OF ORIGIN Eastern Mediterranean
WILD HABITAT A coastal and island species,
growing in rocky areas
HOME HABITAT Cool rooms, such as
bedrooms, porches, hallways
COMMON PROBLEMS Keeping them too
warm shortens the flowering season, and makes
the foliage go yellow; rotting of the crown is
due to excessive watering

The commonly grown cyclamens are hybrids of
Cyclamen persicum, which have been bred to
produce fleshy leaves and large flowers. They
live in cool, damp conditions in the winter and
intense sunlight and heat in the summer. These
conditions are needed in the home, but the
trouble is that most cyclamens are thrown out
needlessly after flowering because they seem to
die. In fact, they can be kept alive for up to
40 years.

A cool room, ideally 10–16°C (50–60°F),
such as a hallway or bedroom, is essential to
keep the plant flowering in winter and spring.
It cannot stand frost, but on the other hand, if
the temperature is too warm the flowers droop
and the plant gradually dies because it 'thinks' it
is summertime and prepares to go into its rest
period as it does in the wild. In a warm lounge
it will probably only flower for about two
weeks.

To keep a cyclamen flowering over several
years, the plant needs to be dried out after
flowering when it dies down, and stored in a
cool dry place, such as in a cupboard.
Alternatively, the pot can be laid on its side
outdoors or planted in a dry, slug-free part of
the garden. After a month or two it can
gradually be rewatered but needs to be kept
cool, and if kept outdoors it should be brought
back inside at the end of September. Even
though the corm may have been completely
dried out, and all the leaves have died, it
will come back to life and new buds will
form.

New plants are best bought in autumn, with
unopened buds, to give the plants time to
acclimatize to the home environment, and if
kept cool the plant could flower through the
winter and early spring. By manipulating light
and temperature, commercial growers produce
flowering cyclamens almost throughout the
year, except during June and July.

Some species of cyclamen are endangered in
the wild. During the 1980s, for example, 50
million cyclamens and other bulb plants were
collected each year from Turkey. The situation
is improving, with better controls on wild
collecting and with schemes for local farmers to
propagate bulbs on farms. Most of the bulb
industry does take a very responsible attitude,
but if you are thinking of growing species other
than the common *Cyclamen persicum* hybrids
from corms then the packet should be labelled
'Bulbs grown from cultivated stock'. Cyclamens
can be grown from seed in late summer
but it takes nearly two years to come into
flower.

Cymbidium
See also ORCHIDS

The easiest orchids to grow as house plants are
the cymbidiums. They are fairly easy and cheap
to buy, very long lasting but unfortunately are
difficult to get back into flower for several years
after the first blooming. There are thousands of

PLANTS *Cymbidium* hybrids
REGION OF ORIGIN Australia and Asia,
especially China
WILD HABITAT Tropical lowland and cooler
highland species, epiphytic on trees
HOME HABITAT Bright position on east- or
west-facing windowsill
COMMON PROBLEMS No flowering is most
often due to lack of light or not following the
culture conditions; limp growth can be due to
lack of light; in cool rooms too much misting
and watering can cause fungus and rot

---

hybrids available for growing at home but the miniature ones with upright flower spikes are the best ones to grow on a windowsill.

In the wild they are found in Asia and Australia, and grow largely as epiphytes, perched on trees above the ground. Without roots in the ground they have to cope with intermittent shortages of water and they have adapted to these droughts by using swollen stems to store food and water.

Like most orchids, you need to get their feeding and light right. Most growers treat them as ground-dwelling plants, but respect their natural epiphyte habits, putting them in a pot with very porous compost made from mixtures such as bark fibre, vermiculate, moss and washed shell grit. From May onwards, when there is more light, they can be fed every two to three weeks with liquid fertilizer, and they need to be kept moist by spraying and placing over a damp pebble tray. During the summer they grow leaves and look quite uninteresting, and they can even be put outdoors (or in a greenhouse if you have one), but they need the bright dappled light they would get in the canopy of trees and not direct sunlight. When frosts threaten in autumn they need to be brought back indoors to a warm room, but cool at night, about 13 – 16°C (55 – 60°F), and they should be placed in a very bright position, such as an east-facing window, or south-facing with some sun-screening from a net curtain. The orchid blooms in winter, and flowers best when potbound, so leave it in its original pot. The plant needs misting but only a little direct watering just to keep the compost moist. When you get to know the plant you can tell how much water it has just by picking up the pot and feeling its weight.

The *Cymbidium* orchids are probably some of the oldest recorded orchids and were mentioned in Chinese herbals from about 200 BC: 'the thickened root when boiled in water and mixed with fermented glutinous rice, is said to be good for curing stomach ache.'

Cyperus
[Umbrella plant]

This is a plant of African wetlands, such as marshes, ditches, and riverbanks, where it enjoys plenty of water. That's one reason why *Cyperus* is so easy to look after because it is almost impossible to overwater, provided its stems are kept dry.

The plant survives waterlogging because it has its own internal ventilation system. The stem and roots are a labyrinth of air-filled channels which act like snorkels, letting oxygen diffuse down into the waterlogged roots and preventing them from being 'suffocated' and rotting.

The other growing conditions they like are humid, warm, shady places which you might find on a bathroom or kitchen windowsill. Because they come from semi-tropical and tropical regions they thrive best in moderately

Cyperus alternifolius

> **PLANTS** *Cyperus alternifolius*
> **REGION OF ORIGIN** Africa
> **WILD HABITAT** Marshes, riverbanks, wetlands
> **HOME HABITAT** Very versatile, but not in strong sunlight; bathrooms and kitchens are good
> **COMMON PROBLEM** Strong sunlight burns the leaves

warm rooms, at about 13–18°C (55–65°F). And because they usually grow in fairly fertile soils the house plants appreciate a regular feed of fertilizer.

Cyperus can be grown in a water-filled jar with a small amount of sandy soil, about 5 cm (2 in), weighted down by a thin layer of gravel. Tall glass spaghetti jars, about 30 cm (1 ft) high are best, and although the water level isn't critical – about a quarter full will do – it is easy to see when they need topping up. Even if the plant completely dries out it will survive for a short time, just as it would in its wild habitat when the small streams occasionally dry out. However, any parts that look like straw will not recover.

The umbrella plant is a sedge, related to grasses and rushes and what look like its leaves, the spokes of the 'umbrella', are in fact bracts surrounding a grasslike flower-head. The true leaves are tiny and are at the base of the stem. The heads of the plant are well adapted for propagation because tall stands of *Cyperus* flop over so that the umbrella part of the shoot bends and snaps off, and floats into the stream or river it has been growing alongside. It then lodges somewhere else, takes root and grows into a new plant.

So the best way to propagate a plant is to cut off one of the umbrellas, the leaf stalk and its spread of bracts. Curiously, if the umbrella is put upside down in a bottle of water a young plant will grow upside down from the umbrella. This may seem strange but as they grow naturally in marshes and by waterways, and the

plants bow down towards the water, new shoots can often be submerged. But the new plants will eventually reach the surface and float away to make a new colony.

The umbrella plant grows up to 1 m (3 ft) tall, but a close relative of it grows much taller. The papyrus plant, *Cyperus papyrus*, was first used by the ancient Egyptians about 5000 years ago for making writing material, and as a house plant it will grow up to 3 m (10 ft) tall in a living room, which makes a spectacular display! It too needs wet growing conditions, and apart from its size makes an easy house plant to grow.

Daffodil

[*Narcissus*]

Keeping daffodils indoors is becoming increasingly common in Britain; in 1993 over two hundred thousand pots of the miniature *Narcissus cyclamineus* 'Tête-à-Tête' variety were sold. There isn't really any difference between a daffodil and a narcissus, though people call the plant 'daffodil' when the central trumpet of the flower is long.

Daffodils are natives of Europe, North Africa and Asia and are one of the few pot plants that grow naturally in Britain, in open forests from Devon to Gloucestershire and the Lake District. To collect them from the wild, however, is illegal and unnecessary as there are so many hybrids from which to choose. The wild variety is paler and much shorter than the highly bred

> **PLANTS** *Narcissus hybrida, Narcissus tazetta,* etc.
> **REGION OF ORIGIN** Europe, Mediterranean, North Africa
> **WILD HABITAT** Open temperate forest
> **HOME HABITAT** A temporary resident of cool bright rooms such as bedrooms
> **COMMON PROBLEMS** Wilting due to heat, move to cooler location and keep watered

garden varieties such as *Narcissus hybrida* 'King Alfred'.

Since they are really plants 'borrowed' from outdoors, during flowering they are best kept well watered and cool, 10°C (50°F), in a porch or unheated bedroom for example, and returned to the garden afterwards. All the outdoor varieties can be grown in pots but some of the best are the small 'Tazettas' which produce bunches of delicate white flowers at Christmas time. Potted daffodils just coming into bud can be bought throughout spring, or daffodils can be potted up in the autumn (starting in September for the earliest flowering) using bulb fibre or a well-drained mixture of sand and potting compost. The bulbs shouldn't be pushed into the soil as bruising could help rot to set in; instead they should be set on a layer of compost in the bottom of the bowl, and have the rest of the compost put on top. The correct depth is about twice the circumference of the bulbs.

The Victorians prolonged their flowering displays by replacing plants which had finished flowering with a succession of new ones brought in from outside.

Darlingtonia

[Cobra lily]

See also CARNIVOROUS PLANTS

This is one of the most glorious of all the carnivorous pitcher plants. Like its close cousins the sarracenias, the *Darlingtonia* pitcher grows up as a cornet from the ground, reaching over half a metre (2 ft) tall. But instead of a simple lid over the pitcher entrance, like a sarracenia, it has a highly elaborate cobra-shaped hood.

The pitcher grows naturally in the cool boggy wetlands of California, so as a house plant it needs a good supply of acidic or neutral water, such as rain-water, distilled water or water from a defrosted fridge. Not only that, it is naturally watered by icy cold mountain streams, and needs 'cold feet' to be successful –

PLANTS *Darlingtonia*
REGION OF ORIGIN California, USA
WILD HABITAT Boglands
HOME HABITAT Large sunny windowsill
COMMON PROBLEMS Tap-water kills the plant – it needs plenty of acid or neutral water

one of the rare plants that prefers being watered with cold water! Apart from having cold roots, the plant itself does best at cooler temperatures below about 18°C (65°F). It should never be allowed to dry out, and in the summer can be stood in a shallow bucket of water. Because the wetlands *Darlingtonia* comes from are poor in nutrients, the plant doesn't need artificial feeds, and it can be grown in live sphagnum moss rather than soil.

The trap works like a lobster pot. An insect crawling into the pitcher finds it easy to get in but the hood makes it very difficult to get out. Its disorientation is made worse by translucent patches in the hood which appear like windows to the creature inside, and as it frantically bangs its head trying to escape it exhausts itself and falls into the deadly digestive bath at the base of the pitcher.

Date palms

[*Phoenix*]

Date palms mostly come from Africa. They have a reputation for growing in intense sunshine in almost drought conditions, but the young plants are shaded because they grow as suckers from the base of the parent palm. As house plants, date palms need good soakings of water in the summer growing season, although they hardly need watering during winter when they are resting.

Being plants of arid lands they have vigorous root systems which grow deep in search of water. So as house plants they need good crocking in the bottom of their pots to help

---

PLANTS *Phoenix*
REGION OF ORIGIN Africa and Asia
WILD HABITAT Mostly from arid regions
HOME HABITAT Warm rooms
COMMON PROBLEMS Too little light causes floppy, elongated fronds; brown/white split-pea sized scale bugs which can be removed from stems and leaves by dabbing with methylated spirit

---

stop the roots growing through and blocking the drainage hole.

A myth about date palms is that they need to be kept warm all the year round. In their native habitats they are used to cool winters, so the common date palm (*Phoenix dactylifera*) and its close cousin the Canary date palm (*Phoenix canariensis*) both need to be kept cooler in winter, down to about 8°C (46°F). If you are short of space at home, there is a miniature date palm from the South China seas, *Phoenix roebelenii*, which can be grown as a house plant although it needs tropical temperatures and more humidity than the other *Phoenix* species.

Date palms can be grown from date stones, but it takes about two years for the stone to produce a single grass-like shoot. The stones should be left to rot down with their fleshy parts, buried just below the surface of warm compost at about 18°C (65°F). It is sobering to think that this little date stone can become a 3 tonne tree in its natural habitat.

The Greek name *Phoenix* means purple or red, and may refer to the reddish fruits of the date palm, or to the Phoenicians who widely cultivated dates and were famous for their red and purple dyes. Plants of the date palm are either male or female and there are Assyrian frieze drawings from about 5000 BC which depict hand pollination of date palms, one of the first recorded pieces of horticulture!

Dendrobium

See also ORCHIDS

These are rock-growing or epiphytic plants perched on trees for support. They need good light but not direct sunlight, plenty of water and fertilizer while growing, but to understand more of their needs you must know something of their natural backgrounds.

Species from India and Australia need to be kept cool and dry in the winter in order to flower the following year. Species from more tropical parts require moisture throughout the year and a minimum winter temperature of 18°C (65°F) to flower well. Many species from high altitudes also need moisture throughout the year, cooler temperatures and shading in summer. Most dendrobiums flower in spring, but it is not a general rule because some species such as *Dendrobium findlayanum*, from the mountains of Burma and Thailand, flower in late summer and others, such as *Dendrobium formosum*, from the Himalayas, Burma and Thailand, flower in late winter.

Cool-growing species which require a winter dry period include the robust *Dendrobium nobilis* with white and red or pink or purple flowers which blooms in winter and early spring.

Cool-growing species which require moisture throughout the year include many with brightly coloured flowers from the cool highlands of New Guinea: examples are *Dendrobium cuthbertsonii* and *Dendrobium lawesii*.

PLANTS *Dendrobium*
REGION OF ORIGIN Range of tropical regions of Asia
WILD HABITAT Rocks or tree perches
HOME HABITAT Living room
COMMON PROBLEMS Rot in winter caused by watering

Dicksonia

See Tree ferns

Dieffenbachia
[Dumb cane]

See also AROIDS

Dieffenbachia comes from south and central America with one species in the West Indies. *Dieffenbachia* grows in classic 'Tarzan jungle': warm, humid, and shady on the forest floor. So the house plant appreciates being in a half-shaded place out of direct bright sunlight, watered well in summer and misted with water spray. However, you can tell if they don't get enough light because they start losing their characteristic dappled leaf markings. There are many hybrids, mainly of the species *Dieffenbachia amoena*, with different degrees of variegation from lightly speckled to almost completely cream. But despite their tropical heritage, dieffenbachias can cope with cool temperatures down to a minimum of about 6–10°C (43–50°F).

Although *Dieffenbachia* is a house plant it can be dangerous. The leaves contain thousands of fine, needle-like crystals of calcium oxalate which pierce the mouth if eaten and once that happens a poison in the leaf inflames the mouth so quickly the tongue swells up and stops any speech – hence its common name dumb cane. In severe cases, the swelling is so bad that it can cause asphyxiation, but in practice it is children and pets that are at greatest risk from *Dieffenbachia* poisoning. You also need to be careful about handling it when, for example, trying to propagate the plant from tip cuttings.

The plant is named after Joseph Dieffenbach, head gardener at the imperial palace of Schönbrunn, in Vienna in the 1830s.

Dionaea muscipula
See Venus flytrap

Dracaena

Dracaenas are native to large parts of tropical and sub-tropical Africa and the Canary Islands. They grow in savanna woodland as upright-growing shrubs, in four to five years reaching over a metre (3 ft) tall. As house plants they are exceptionally tough and easy to grow, although it's often a good idea to raise the humidity around them by, for example, standing them on a tray of moist pebbles. They have got an unfortunate tendency to lose leaves from the bottom of their stems, but don't worry because this is normal and gives the plant an attractive palm-like appearance. One of their other virtues is that dracaenas are virtually immune to pests.

Dracaena fragrans is one of the tougher species, coming from Upper Guinea, but the less frequently available *Dracaena goldieana*, from the same country, demands high and constant temperatures and humidity. *Dracaena marginata* comes from Madagascar and is a very

---

PLANTS *Dieffenbachia*
REGION OF ORIGIN Latin America
WILD HABITAT Tropical rainforest – humid, warm, filtered light
HOME HABITAT Half-shaded living room out of direct sunlight
COMMON PROBLEMS Not enough light, which leads to leggy plants and loss of variegation; and sudden temperature changes which can cause leaf collapse and fall, as can overwatering which will also eventually rot the stem

---

PLANTS *Dracaena fragrans*
REGION OF ORIGIN Upper Guinea
WILD HABITAT In grassy woodland as a shrub
HOME HABITAT In large kitchen or bathroom; most species enjoy regular misting and/or damp pebble tray
COMMON PROBLEMS Leaves can wither and die in dry air; some dracaenas can be sensitive to fluorine in water shown as brown 'chemical' stains on the leaves – use rain-water; too much watering causes root rot

PLANTS *Dracaena draco*
REGION OF ORIGIN Canary Islands
WILD HABITAT Dry, semi-arid plains and scrubland
HOME HABITAT Can take cool temperatures, needs a large room, so good for offices and in the home in bedrooms, dining rooms and hallways
COMMON PROBLEMS A very tough plant with few problems, except for brown leaves from under- or overwatering, leading to root rot; fluoride or chlorine in the water can damage the plant

popular house plant, needing plenty of watering during its growing season and more humidity.

Dracaena draco, the dragon tree of the Canary Islands, is the toughest dracaena of cooler regions but needs plenty of watering during its growing season, although it can survive in dry air without misting. It likes reasonably good light and in winter a cool room at about 13 – 18°C (55 – 65°F), such as a bedroom or dining room, but it can stretch to cooler or warmer conditions. It should be regularly fed with fertilizer and water during the growing season but it doesn't die even after some neglect. Coming from a semi-tropical environment it also needs a winter rest with much less watering and fertilizing.

Dracaenas are closely allied to the cordylines and yuccas; in fact several of the species have been confused and *Cordyline australis* was originally classified as *Dracaena australis*.

Drosera
See Sundews

Dumb cane
See *Dieffenbachia*

Dwarf coconut palm
See *Microcoelum*

Echinocactus, Ferocactus
[Golden barrel cactus and barrel cactus]
See also CACTI

These two cacti are very common in the deserts of south-west USA and Mexico, easily identified by their barrel shape, ferocious curved spines and deep ridges. These ridges are interesting because they operate like a concertina: during our winter the cactus rests without water, and the ridges deepen; but when the plant is rewatered in springtime, the cactus inflates with water and the ridges collapse. Without the ridges, the skin of the cactus might easily split, but they also have another function. As the sunlight moves round the cactus during the day, the ridges – and also the spines – help shade the cactus body. In the wild large bell-shaped flowers appear at the top of mature plants some feet high, but in cultivation these are seldom seen.

Like all cacti, *Ferocactus* needs watering during the spring and summer, and rest without

Echinocactus grusonii

PLANTS *Echinocactus* and *Ferocactus*
REGION OF ORIGIN South-west USA and
Mexico
WILD HABITAT Deserts
HOME HABITAT Sunny living room
windowsills in summer, cool bedroom in
winter
COMMON PROBLEMS Watering in winter
causes rot

water in the winter. It also enjoys resting in a
cool, about 5°C (41°F) place without getting
frozen. During the summer it enjoys a bright
sunny windowsill, and the light helps to colour
the spines red, but in the winter it can be
moved to a table near a window in a cool
bedroom.

Ferox is the Latin for fierce and the name
means 'fierce cactus', which you may remember
if you accidentally sit on one!

Epipremnum

See also AROIDS

These are aroid plant climbers, with variegated
leaves, growing in the humid rainforests of
Malaysia, the Solomon Islands and Indonesia.
They clamber up trees with aerial roots and,
like the Swiss cheese plant, when potted they
prefer a moss pole to climb up.

Epipremnum aureum is the most common
house plant species, but it has lots of synonyms,
scientific and common: *Pothos aureus,*

PLANT *Epipremnum*
REGION OF ORIGIN South-east Asia,
Indian Ocean
WILD HABITAT Tropical rainforests
HOME HABITAT Living room with moderate
shade, humid, warm
COMMON PROBLEMS Waterlogging
causes stems to rot; leaves curl and die from
sudden chill; highly variegated types need
more light

Epipremnum aureum

Raphidophora aurea, Scindapsus aureus; ivy arum, devil's ivy, golden pothos.

Since the plant grows for a large part of its life under the canopy of trees, it does not need direct sunlight and can grow well in a shady corner, although the highly variegated types need slightly more light. It must be kept humid with, for example, regular spraying and by its standing on a tray of damp pebbles, but it doesn't like a waterlogged soil and should only be watered liberally in spring and summer. It enjoys warm temperatures, but can survive down to about 12°C (54°F) in its winter resting period; at these temperatures it also needs less water. In fact, *Epipremnum* is a very tough plant, very difficult to kill, which makes it ideal for living rooms.

One interesting phenomenon worth looking out for in a thriving *Epipremnum aureum* is the way it changes leaf shape just before it is about to flower. The normally small undivided leaves turn into a large lobed leaf 60 cm (24 in) or more in diameter. In the wild this happens when the climber reaches the light at the top of a tree, so you could try letting the plant grow up into the light of a window.

The house plant rarely flowers but when it isn't flowering *Epipremnum* is easily grown from cuttings about 10 cm (4 in) long taken from the tip of the shoot, especially if they are dipped in rooting hormone, available at garden shops. The shoots will even grow in water.

Euphorbia

See also POINSETTIA

There are over 2000 species of *Euphorbia*, from all over the temperate and tropical world, but the commonest house plants are poinsettia (*Euphorbia pulcherrima*) from the humid mountains of Mexico (described under its own

---

Euphorbia are succulents adapted to drought from all over the temperate and tropical world, including the popular Poinsettia and Crown of thorns.

PLANTS *Euphorbia milii*
REGION OF ORIGIN Madagascar
WILD HABITAT Tropical drylands
HOME HABITAT Almost anywhere dry and hot
COMMON PROBLEMS Leaf drop from overwatering or moving the plant

---

heading) and *Euphorbia milii* (crown of thorns) from Madagascar.

Crown of thorns is one of those rare house plants that you can thoroughly abuse and neglect. It's at home in the hot dry atmosphere of a centrally heated home, can even be stood next to a radiator, and flowers almost throughout the year with small flowers surrounded by beautiful red bracts. It hardly needs much attention apart from occasional watering, a weak fertilizer during the summer growing season, and sunlight. It doesn't like being moved or overwatered, otherwise it drops its leaves, although it has the disturbing habit of dropping its withered old leaves in any case.

A couple of cautions, though. It is covered in sharp thorns, and its milky sap is poisonous, so plants need to be kept out of reach of children and pets. The common name for *Euphorbia milii* comes from the idea that it was the plant placed on the head of Christ during crucifixion.

Exacum

At first sight *Exacum* looks as though it is a mutant variety of miniature African violet, having star-shaped purple flowers. But *Exacum affine* is a distinct species of its own from the gentian family. It is a native from the coastal regions of the semi-arid island of Socotra, on the horn of Africa opposite Somalia.

It does not survive more than a season, although *Exacum* flowers from mid-summer to late autumn, especially if the dead flowers are removed. Although it is considered a 'throw-

PLANTS *Exacum affine*
REGION OF ORIGIN Socotra Island, Africa
WILD HABITAT Low-growing plant in coastal scrub
HOME HABITAT Bright cool location such as bedroom
COMMON PROBLEMS Wilting due to lack of water; flowering can be prolonged by picking off dead flowers

away' plant after flowering, the slightly fragrant and delicate flowers are considered worth the effort. The plants can be raised from seed in a soil-based mixture and need to be kept well watered. Exacums enjoy bright light and cool temperatures below 21°C (70°F).

Fatshedera

Fatshedera has a pioneering place in house plant history because it was one of the first hybrid plants to be produced by a cross between species from two different genera: the European ivy, *Hedera helix* 'Hibernica', crossed with *Fatsia japonica* 'Moseri', a castor oil plant from the temperate forests of Japan. It was achieved by the French tree growers, the Lizé brothers at their nursery in Nantes and was first marketed in 1912. This sort of 'bigeneric' cross is rare except among the orchids.

These plants get the best of both worlds because they have the broad spread of the castor oil plant and the climbing habit of ivy. Though the stem of the hybrid is strong, it still needs supports and usually two or three plants are put in each pot to make an excellent display. Today there are at least four varieties produced in large numbers by the Dutch plant industry, for example: *Fatshedera lizei* 'Annemieke', a wide-leafed variety with subtle dark leaf marks, and *Fatshedera lizei* 'Pia', a tall compact hybrid with small leaves. If they grow too thin, their climbing can be curtailed by pinching out the

Exacum affine

PLANTS *Fatshedera*, artificial cross between *Fatsia* and *Hedera*
REGION OF ORIGIN *Fatsia* from Japan and *Hedera* from Europe
WILD HABITAT Open temperate forests (both ivy and castor oil plant)
HOME HABITAT Cool, shady or light rooms
COMMON PROBLEMS Too little water damages the leaves; standing in water makes the lower leaves fall off; red spider mite can attack if too dry but misting should prevent and cure

FERNS included in this book:
Asplenium nidus (bird's nest fern)
Hare's foot fern (*Polypodium aureum*)
Hart's tongue fern (*Phyllitis scolopendrium*)
Maidenhair fern (*Adiantum*)
Nephrolepis (ladder fern)
Stag's horn fern (*Platycerium*)
Tree ferns (*Dicksonia* and *Cyathea*)

growing tips in spring, and they can stand quite drastic pruning. Real ivy can be grafted into the leaf joints, and makes a strange looking cascade around the stem.

Fatsias grow in the temperate mountain oak forests of Japan where the ground cover is a thin layer of grass, laurel and other shrubs. It is not a dense dark forest, so it is not surprising that *Fatshedera*, although it can stand a little shade, benefits from brighter light, especially in winter. Minimum winter temperature 45°F (7°C).

Like ivy, *Fatshedera* needs to be kept well watered, especially in summer. A good soaking is a substitute for Japan's summer monsoon!

FERNS

The origins of ferns are older than dinosaurs, and much older than the flowering plants, and many are still some of the most successful plants on earth.

Instead of flowers and seeds the underneath of most fern fronds have small brown powdery bumps called sporangia. These hold spores which are blown by the wind to new homes where each spore germinates into a small flat leaf-like plate called a prothallus. This is the sexual part of the fern, and under each prothallus are the sex organs where after fertilization, a new fern plant develops. If you

sow fern spores the small ferns all look the same to begin with, and differences between the species begin to appear in the third and fourth years.

Ferns tend to be well adapted to low light conditions, living as forest floor plants or hiding in damp rocky crevices. Some ferns are extremely shady plants and hardly need any light at all, such as the filmy ferns which have very thin fronds only one cell thick and intercept light from any angle. But the problem with growing these is that they dry out in minutes in dry air, so they must be grown in a tightly enclosed container like a terrarium. As a rule of thumb, the more ferns are adapted to the shade the more they need humidity and the less they tolerate wind and draughts. This can

Nephrolepis

make them fragile and delicate and therefore very difficult to cultivate.

Generally speaking, ferns from the most sheltered forest floor sites often have more finely divided and bigger fronds than those of other, more open-living species, and they enjoy a wind-free environment.

Ferns have been cultivated since medieval times when they were valued for their use in medicine, and there was an enormous craze for growing them in the Victorian era when they were grown in glass tanks called Wardian cases.

Ficus benjamina
[Weeping fig]

Ficus benjamina is widespread in the humid tropical forests of south and south-east Asia as well as Australia. This type of *Ficus* has become a very popular pot plant of recent years in the home and office.

Even though it's not quite the tough plant it is made out to be, people often find it difficult to grow because it is always dropping leaves. In the wild they drop their leaves in the dry season, and replace them with growth at the tips of their branches, so some undramatic leaf shedding is normal. But in the house, away from light, in dry and hot air they can suffer massive leaf drop because of stress. They drop leaves especially on the side away from light, so plants need to be put closer to a window during winter and turned regularly so that all sides receive light. The intense heat of a nearby radiator also causes leaf drop but so do sudden temperature drops below about 10°C (50°F) and they shouldn't be trapped between the window and curtain at night in winter. Happily, even after a catastrophic leaf drop they can recover if removed to a more suitable location. It is best not to put them through all this trauma because, even if they do survive, their growth will be checked for many months. In a hallway they might get light from above or from other rooms, producing an eye-catching tree-like growth.

Ficus benjamina

Although we grow *F. benjamina* as a popular weeping fig, with delicate drooping growth and willow-like leaves, in the wild it grows as a so-called strangling fig. The seeds are first dropped into the tops of trees by bats, birds, monkeys or squirrels. At first the young fig grows purely as an epiphyte (growing out of contact with the ground) in debris lodged in the bark. The fig

PLANTS *Ficus benjamina*
REGION OF ORIGIN South and south-east Asia, Australia
WILD HABITAT A strangling vine or rainforest tree
HOME HABITAT A bright spot in living room, or lit from a skylight in a hallway
COMMON PROBLEMS Leaf drop due to lack of light or extremes of temperature and humidity

grows roots which cling to the branches of the tree, and as it gets larger the fig sends down long dangling roots towards the ground. Once the roots touch the ground they grow larger and more roots are sent down to the ground, forming an interlacing network that looks like a basket woven around the host tree, and which slowly encases it like a cage. The tree is so tightly encased it can no longer grow in width and becomes slowly 'strangled' and eventually dies, leaving the strangler fig on its own as a root cage up to 30 m (90 ft) tall. For a big tree the strangulation can take about a century to complete. But if the strangling fig germinates on the ground instead of in a treetop it never forms a tall trunk nor has any strangling tendencies, so you've got no worries about growing it as a house plant!

Ficus elastica

[Indian rubber plant]

Small wonder that the Indian rubber plant is one of the most popular house plants, because one of the biggest problems growing it is its extraordinary success! They are exceedingly tough plants; in fact, they're thugs! They can cope with long periods without water, and cold, or bright sun or deep shade makes little difference to them. So they often swamp a room with their thick leathery leaves and come to be such a nuisance that people often prune them back, only to find they grow even lusher. In fact, the harder you prune the more

sideshoots they send out and the more rampant the plant becomes.

But this is no surprise because in their native environment, from India to Malaysia, they grow over a wide range of habitats, from rugged hills to hot sunny lowlands, developing as trees

Ficus elastica 'Tineke'

reaching up to 30 m (100 ft) tall, so a 3-m (9-ft) specimen in the living room is actually quite a baby!

Their other big problem as house plants is an alarming habit of shedding leaves until they eventually become a skeleton of stem and leaf stalks. But this is a perfectly normal response to lack of water. In the wild they often survive several months' drought following the monsoon season, and shedding their leaves is a drastic way of preventing water escaping through the leaf pores. In the home, the way to avoid this leaf fall is to keep the plant reasonably well watered so the soil is moist below its surface, but beware of overwatering because then the leaves turn yellow. Normally the plant is happy to withstand several days without watering, and this is because its leaves are superbly well adapted to storing water. Its leaf pores are sunk into pits to slow down evaporation, and the inside of the leaf is packed full of layers of juicy water-filled cells which act like miniature water tanks.

Another drought adaptation is a special waxy, conical-shaped sheath covering the delicate growing tip of the shoot, to protect the shoot tip from drying up in hot weather. When a new leaf is formed the sheath splits, letting the leaf inside uncurl.

So successful is the Indian rubber plant in the wild that it often grows as a weed, taking root in obscure places like cracks in pavements and derelict sites. This is partly thanks to its superb drought resistance and partly because it has a vigorous root system which searches deep and wide for moisture, and is often strong enough to lift paving stones or crack road surfaces. The plant also has slender sausage-shaped roots which grow out of the stem. These aerial roots grow down into the soil and both support the branches and feed them with water

The Indian rubber plant in the wild grows as a tree adapted to long periods of drought and sudden torrential rain.

PLANTS *Ficus elastica*
REGION OF ORIGIN India to Malaysia
WILD HABITAT Forests to urban areas
HOME HABITAT Almost anywhere with
sufficient room
COMMON PROBLEMS Leaf drop caused by
lack of water; yellow leaves from overwatering

and minerals. In the tropics, the trees are sometimes grown like a rambling trellis, with branches growing out sideways supported on columns of thick aerial root. One tree in India has been grown to cover 4½ hectares (14 acres)!

But the plant also has to cope with the torrential rains of the monsoons, and waterlogging is a big problem for all tropical rainforest trees. Heavy rainfall and humidity leaves a film of water clinging on to the foliage; this can reduce the flow of water through the inside of the tree by choking off the tiny pores in the leaves which normally evaporate water. And because a film of water reflects light, it also cuts down photosynthesis. Nutrients can also be leached by the rain and dampness encourages a range of epiphytes – mosses, lichens, fungi and so on – to grow on the leaves and make the problems even worse. So getting rid of surplus surface water on the leaves is crucial, and trees such as *Ficus* use a neat piece of drainage engineering to cope with the problem. They drain the surface water off the leaves by their long tapering tips which curl downwards and run off the water. Plants growing in wetter areas grow longer and larger drip tips than plants from drier areas.

The Indian rubber plant also copes well with deep shade or bright sunlight. For most plants growing in the tropics they can usually only cope with either one or the other, but the rubber plant's leaves are so versatile they can change their photosynthesis to suit the light levels. This means that a rubber plant will do well in the corner of a room or by a window.

In fact, you would have to be guilty of gross negligence to kill an Indian rubber plant! The conditions they cannot tolerate are complete darkness, cold temperatures approaching freezing, about 5°C (40°F) or below, lack of watering for more than several months, or waterlogged soil. Other than that, beware of vigorous growth!

Ficus pumila
[Creeping or Chinese fig]

This is a thin-leaved *Ficus* from Japan, North Vietnam, Australia and the warmer parts of China. It is very different from the sturdy banyan and rubber trees that also belong to the ficus group, and has lots of small leaves about 2 cm (1 in) long covering its stem. Being used to high temperatures in summer and an average cool of about 10°C (50°F) in winter, it is almost hardy and will survive in very sheltered places outdoors. It roots deeply beneath boulders in China and so it never dries out or gets warm roots.

It is a climbing plant, and is good for trailing and rooting down into moist material which make it very easy to propagate. One of the essentials is to keep the roots well watered, even in winter, otherwise the leaves will shrivel and won't recover when given more water, although new leaves may sprout on the stem. The situation is made worse for the plant in the home when you consider that it grows like ivy in the wild. It climbs with clinging roots which

PLANTS *Ficus pumila*
REGION OF ORIGIN South-east Asia,
Australia
WILD HABITAT An ivy-like creeper in
sub-tropical forest
HOME HABITAT Shady bathroom or dining
room, no direct sun
COMMON PROBLEMS If the roots dry out
the leaves shrivel and die; excessive watering
will cause leaves to fall off

Ficus pumila

PLANTS *Fittonia verschaffeltii,
F. argyroneura* v. 'Minima'
REGION OF ORIGIN Peru
WILD HABITAT Tropical rainforest floor
HOME HABITAT Best in a terrarium
COMMON PROBLEMS Draughts, dry air,
cold temperatures, overwatering and
underwatering can all be fatal

attach firmly to supports, each new set of roots being able to absorb water. In the living room there is just one long trailing piece and it has to rely on its main roots alone.

However, as with the Indian rubber plant, too much water makes the lower leaves fall off, so it needs moderate regular watering during the growing period when the soil surface is dried out. One alternative to growing *F. pumila* as a pot plant is to give it a terrarium where its water needs are well satisfied, and where it is possible for it to creep across the humid soil with several rooted branches. In a greenhouse the plant produces non-climbing stiff flowering stalks.

Fittonia

[Mosaic plant]

Fittonia verschaffeltii comes from the tropical rainforests of Peru. It is a forest-floor, ground-hugging plant which creeps over the ground to form large patches of foliage, but it can also grow over fallen trees, rocks and the lower branches of living trees.

Fittonia has brilliantly marked foliage, but unfortunately it is a very fussy plant to grow, largely because of its natural heritage. In the forest it needs decaying debris or moss for its roots to hold fast, and so the house plant needs to be grown in soil mixed with sand kept in well-crocked pots for good drainage. It also needs warmth, high humidity and regular rainfall. Ironically, it is easy to overwater the house plant probably because the wild plant is used to well drained, very shallow leaf litter soil on the forest floor. Overwatering makes the plant stems rot and leaves curl and shrivel – they should be kept moist and no more. Misting of the leaves can also cause rot if the spray is too vigorous, but dry air will kill so a damp pebble tray beneath the pot is helpful.

Being a tropical plant *Fittonia* needs a minimum warmth of about 13–16°C (55–60°F) and sudden or large swings in temperature are harmful. In low temperatures the growth slows and the plant can become sick – the leaves become small and turn white.

Another feature of the tropical rainforest is its craving for shade and humidity. So it is probably best grown in a terrarium where the humidity and temperature can be kept constantly high, especially during winter. The small-leaved variety, *Fittonia argyroneura* var. 'Minima', can even be grown in a bottle. The 'Minima' variety's leaves are between 2–3 cm (about 0.5–1 in) long while those of *F. verschaffeltii* are 7–10 cm (3–4 in) long.

Fittonia argyroneura

A successful *Fittonia* plant will elongate by creepers and then gets straggly so you have to prune and repropagate it.

Being used to living in the shade of forest floors, *Fittonia* has evolved highly specialized leaf lenses – biconvex lens cells with a very convex outer and more gently curved inner wall to help scavenge for light and reflect it down into the photosynthesizing cells inside the leaf.

The fittonias are named after Elizabeth and Mary Fitton who wrote *Conversations in Botany* in 1817.

Flamingo flower

See *Anthurium*

Gardenia

This very large genus of about 250 bushy plants, part of the same family as coffee, has one good house plant, *Gardenia jasminoides*, the Cape jasmine. Gardenias in general come from the warm and humid deciduous forests of Asia and

> **PLANTS** *Gardenia jasminoides*
> **REGION OF ORIGIN** Southern China
> **WILD HABITAT** Growing as a bush in sub-tropical forest
> **HOME HABITAT** Bright living room, warm and sunny
> **COMMON PROBLEMS** Leaf drop due to cold hard water, or generally too cold; in hard-water areas use tepid rain-water

Africa and *G. jasminoides* comes from the sub-tropical forest of southern China. This kind of forest, known as sclerophyllous forest, has many species of oak and chestnut and the ground is dominated by bushes with laurel-like leaves. The original species has simple white flowers with five petals, but semi double or double cultivated varieties are the norm. In full flower, in early autumn, they have an overpowering musky jasmine perfume which made them very popular with the Victorians, who kept them in a welcoming parlour.

In the home they are difficult to grow because they need constant warm temperatures of 23°C (75°F) and humidity and die if watered with cold hard tap-water. They will tolerate lower temperatures as long as the change is gradual. In the wild they grow in soil with a high acidity, and in hard-water areas it is best to use tepid rain-water. They need bright light but not direct sunlight, but you should give the plant regular mistings, being careful not to wet the flowers. It is a good idea in any case to stand the pot on a damp pebble tray. With care *G. jasminoides* can be kept for several years but it will gradually flower less and less; it is best to use older plants for propagation. Stem cuttings can be taken in the spring and will grow in a warm room with the help of rooting hormone.

If *G. jasminoides* causes too much heartache, a closely related and similarly beautiful species, *Mitriostigma axillare*, wild coffee (previously *Gardenia citrodora*) could be tried, but you will probably have to ask your garden centre to order it in specially. It is slow-growing and therefore expensive for commercial cultivation, so not widely available. *Mitriostigma axillare* comes from South Africa and Natal and is slightly hardier than *G. jasminoides*. The Victorians had great success with this 'African gardenia' and kept it as a windowsill plant.

Gardenias were named after Dr Alexander Garden (1730–1791), a Scottish naturalist.

Geraniums

See *Pelargonium*

Goosefoots

See *Syngonium*

Guzmania

See also BROMELIADS

This is a very successful genus of bromeliads in the wild, ranging northwards from Paraguay right up into Central America, and even Florida. These plants live on trees, sometimes blanketing them in huge clumps, with rosettes of brilliantly coloured leaves branching out from shallow water-filled cups. The most popular varieties are of the species *Guzmania lingulata* which is from Paraguay, Ecuador, Bolivia and high in the mountains of the Colombian Andes. Most guzmanias enjoy warm temperatures between about 18–24°C (65–75°F), and will need this for flowering, but being mountainous tropical species they will tolerate much cooler temperatures, down to about 10°C (50°F).

PLANTS *Guzmania* species
REGION OF ORIGIN Florida to Paraguay
WILD HABITAT Festooning tree trunks and branches in tropical rainforest
HOME HABITAT Bathrooms, kitchens and other humid places with light shade
COMMON PROBLEM Lack of humidity in a heated room, so it must be regularly misted

---

As house plants the best feature of the guzmanias are their brightly coloured red bracts and flowers, which can be produced throughout the year. The cup in the centre of the leaf rosette needs filling up with water in summer, less so in winter when the plant is resting and needs less watering. But the cup water should not be allowed to stagnate in cool conditions at any time of year otherwise the guzmania may rot. In the wild this isn't a problem because the bromeliad lives in the buoyant rainforest climate where constant cycles of evaporation and rain continually empty and refill the cups.

The guzmanias enjoy humidity, and potted plants should be stood on a damp pebble tray and misted regularly. They will also thrive when kept humid on a mossy 'bromeliad tree' – a false tree made of bark and moss. Like all bromeliads, it dies, sadly, after flowering, although new plants can be grown from the plantlets at the base of the leaf rosette – but make sure the new plantlets have already grown some tiny roots before they are removed to new pots. Alternatively, they can just be left next to the parent plant which will eventually rot back.

The genus is named in honour of the eighteenth-century Spanish botanist A. Guzman. One brilliant yellow and red species from Costa Rica, *Guzmania zahnii*, is named after Gottlieb Zahn, a fern collector who worked as a collector for the nurseries of Veitch in Exeter. He was unfortunately drowned on one of his collecting expeditions in 1870.

Gymnocalycium

See also CACTI

This is a genus of about 40 to 60 species of cacti from South America. The plants are globular with rounded ribs and varied forms of spines, and have become a very popular supermarket plant. *Gymnocalycium* flowers are very striking white or pale pink and sometimes red or yellow in some species, produced from the top of the stem and remaining open for

PLANTS *Gymnocalycium*
REGION OF ORIGIN South America
WILD HABITAT Arid lands
HOME HABITAT Sunny windowsill, ideal for a living room, moving to cool bedroom come winter
COMMON PROBLEMS Watering during the rest period in winter causing rot or straggly growth

several days. They are sometimes known as 'red caps' or 'yellow caps', depending on species, because it has become popular to graft the flowering caps of the stem on to the body of another cactus.

These are good plants for beginners to grow because they are undemanding plants and free-flowering. In the wild, *Gymnocalycium* often shelters behind boulders or other plants for shade, so protection from blazing sun is advised for the house plant and an indoor windowsill without direct midday sun is satisfactory. Like most cacti, they need a good rest over winter in a cool, dry, light room without water so that they grow well and flower the next season.

Hare's foot fern

[*Polypodium aureum*]

See also FERNS

Polypodium ferns can be found worldwide, but the house plant *Polypodium aureum* is a native

PLANTS *Polypodium aureum*
REGION OF ORIGIN Central and South America, Australia
WILD HABITAT Sub-tropical rainforest, growing on trees or creeping over the ground
HOME HABITAT Living room on pebble tray away from direct light, but better in bathroom or cool bedroom
COMMON PROBLEMS Yellowing fronds if near radiator or in direct sun or if air too dry; move to cooler location and mist

of sub-tropical and tropical forests, from Florida to Argentina and Australia. Growing from an underground stem (rhizome), it crawls over the surface and edges of a pot mixture, so large shallow containers are best to cope with this habit. In the wild it is epiphytic and perches on trees, but it also creeps over the ground.

It has leaves with a deep central groove and is covered with furry brown hair and silvery scales. The hare's foot needs plenty of water during its growing season, but don't go too crazy or it will rot. The plant can survive in the moderately dry air of a living room, though misting and damp pebble trays are helpful. Hare's foot fern doesn't need especially high temperatures but it is best kept above about 10°C (50°F). Some varieties have very attractive undulating edges to the fronds such as *Polypodium aureum* var. 'Mandaianum' which is also beautifully coloured dark green with a hint of blue.

Hart's tongue fern

[*Phyllitis scolopendrium*]

See also FERNS

The hart's tongue fern is one of the few house plants which comes from our own temperate climate, and grows wild mainly in west and south-west Britain, tucked into damp crevices on walls and beneath hedgerows. It is also a native over a wide part of Europe and North America, and because it is temperate it is very

PLANTS *Phyllitis scolopendrium*
REGION OF ORIGIN Europe and North America
WILD HABITAT Woods, hedgerows, rocks, walls
HOME HABITAT Bottle garden, terrarium, cool conservatory or cool humid bathroom or kitchen
COMMON PROBLEMS Lack of moisture can be fatal; very low light stunts growth

tolerant of a wide range of temperature, but prefers cool conditions at about 10–16°C (50–61°F), and dies back in severe frosts. The hart's tongue also tolerates a wide range of light levels, but should not be put in direct sunlight nor in complete shade since it is used to the dappled but bright light of open forest.

Most importantly it does need constant moisture in its soil and enjoys humid air, so it is often grown in a bottle garden, or conservatory or terrarium. Alternatively extra humidity can be obtained by standing it on a damp pebble tray and misting regularly.

Hedera
See Ivy

Hibiscus

Hibiscus species are found all over tropical Asia, and the ornamental varieties have been introduced to many warm countries where they thrive as garden shrubs. In Mauritius, for example, they are planted to beautify the roadsides in the same way that foxgloves have been seeded on the banks of some British motorways. One agricultural species, *Hibiscus esculentus*, provides the widely eaten vegetable, okra.

Hibiscus rosa-sinensis is the species most commonly grown as a house plant. The species grows as a large shrub in the Malaysian lowlands and many other parts of Asia. But it can also be a very successful house plant, lasting for decades on a sunny windowsill as long as it doesn't get too hot. Bright light is important for flowering. It can be severely pruned in early spring to keep it small and bushy, but because it is able to grow so big *Hibiscus* needs regular liquid feeds of high potash and standard fertilizer. The soil-based compost should not be allowed to dry out, otherwise the leaves will drop, and it is a good idea to stand the plant in a damp pebble tray. Sudden temperature changes also can cause the leaves to drop and so

---

PLANTS *Hibiscus rosa-sinensis*
REGION OF ORIGIN Tropical Asia
WILD HABITAT Large shrub in tropical forest
HOME HABITAT Sunny east- or west-facing windowsill
COMMON PROBLEMS Drying out as well as watering with cold water and sudden temperature drops causes leaf and bud fall; prone to aphid attack which requires a soapy or chemical spray, or an interesting alternative is that bio-predators called *Aphidolites* are now available to control infestations

---

tepid water should be used for watering, and as a guide 10°C (50°F) is a minimum temperature.

Propagation in the home is usually from stem cuttings taken in late spring, but the seeds of *Hibiscus* show interesting adaptations; some are hairy to catch in the feathers of birds and in some island species the seeds can float so that they are dispersed by sea.

There are many varieties of *Hibiscus rosa-sinensis* such as 'Paramaribo' (large red flowers), and 'Koenig' (yellow flowers), and *Hibiscus rosa-sinensis* 'Cooperi' has variegated foliage. People who grow hibiscus often end up with them for life!

Hippeastrum
[Amaryllis]

The name *Amaryllis* is very confusing. There are two entirely different groups of plants with the same generic name of *Amaryllis*: hippeastrum bulb plants with big trumpet flowers from Latin America and the cultivated belladonna lily, *Amaryllis belladonna* with smaller, more delicate pink trumpet flowers from South Africa. Hippeastrum is by far the most commonly grown house plant and that's what is described here.

There are about 75 species of wild hippeastrums from Central and South America, and hundreds of hybrids have been bred since the Victorians first recognized their potential as house plants. The modern stock probably originated from bulbs of *Hippeastrum leopoldii*, collected by Richard Pearce in Bolivia during 1863. The hybrids have been bred with stunningly large trumpet flowers in a wide range of colours, including the red 'Cardinal' and white 'Ludwig's Dazzler'.

This is a plant which actually benefits from a small pot. If the roots are given plenty of room, the hippeastrums will grow plenty of leaves but

PLANTS *Hippeastrum leopoldii, H. × ackermanni.* etc.
REGION OF ORIGIN Peru, Bolivia
WILD HABITAT Semi-dry and open tropical forest
HOME HABITAT Bright living room windowsill
COMMON PROBLEMS Bulb will not flower in second year because it hasn't been given a dry rest period

will be reluctant to bloom. Yet when their roots are cramped their instinct is to flower.

In their natural habitat in open forests, hippeastrums are used to dry and wet seasons. The dry period is the plant's resting season which it needs before flowering, so in the home keeping the bulbs dry during autumn and winter often stimulates flowering the following spring. After flowering the plant dies back in late August and the bulb should be stored in a warm, dry place until January, simulating the open sunny places in the wild where the dry bulb ripens and encourages flowering during the following year in the wet season.

The wet season is the signal for the bulb to flower, and in the home it is recreated by repotting the bulb and keeping it warm and watered. Once the flower stalk emerges the bulb needs to be kept cooler which helps the flowers last much longer. Strangely, the leaves emerge after the flowers. Another weird feature is that the hippeastrums are one of the few bulb plants to grow quite naturally with the top of their bulbs exposed above the soil, which just goes to show how very resilient the bulbs are.

Howea forsteriana
[Kentia palm]
See also PALMS

This is the classic Victorian palm of palm court orchestras, and is still the most popular palm today. It comes from one obscure little group of

Hippeastrum amaryllis

islands, the Lord Howe Islands far off the east coast of Australia in the Pacific Ocean, with Kentia their capital. The climate there is airy, breezy, moist and cool to warm, temperate rather than tropical, although the palms are not frost tolerant. The closest equivalent climate in the northern hemisphere is probably the Canary Islands, with a temperature range of about 10–27°C (50–80°F), and they do not do well in tropical conditions.

In the natural habitat kentias can grow up to 13–17 m (40–50 ft) tall. Even though kentias grow as trees, they live under a dense forest cover for much of their lives and only reach sunlight as adults, so they are used to growing in low light, their very dark green leaves making use of the little they receive. This makes them extremely good plants for shady corners of rooms. The tough, leathery, feathery-shaped leaves are also very tolerant of wind, so draughts don't bother them. The plants are also one of the few house plants that it is difficult to kill by overwatering.

So kentia palms are ideal for beginners who think they don't have 'green fingers' or anyone likely to neglect their house plants. But if they do get brown tips to their leaves it could mean one of a number of things: dry air, severe and prolonged drought or drowning in a bucket of water for months on end!

Another attraction of the plant for growing indoors is that it does not take up much space. It is tall and elegant but its leaves are held high, upright and arch over at the top.

Hoya
[Wax plant]

These were the Victorians' favourite buttonholes, with their perfectly formed button-shaped white or pale pink flowers. They also have an attractive red eye which looks like the thread attachment to a button, making the flowers even more appropriate as buttonholes. They come from south China and Australia where they live in tropical rainforests, but they don't need to be kept at a tropical temperature, although they do not enjoy temperatures below about 10°C (50°F) in our winter. There are two commonly cultivated species, *Hoya carnosa* and the more round-leafed *Hoya australis* from Queensland in Australia.

The hoyas have shallow, rather delicate roots used to receiving a lot of air, and as a result must be watered carefully to avoid suffocation. This is because they are epiphytic, perched on other plants, or sometimes trailing and climbing. For the house plant the surface of the compost should be allowed to dry out between waterings, and it is best to use water at room temperature.

The plant makes leaves at the expense of flowers if overfed, but when given a modest liquid fertilizer no more than about once every two weeks, and plenty of light, an attractive ball of about 25 flowers appears. Hoyas grow fast and produce spur stems which should not be removed as they produce flowers in later years. The flowers are especially fragrant at night and

---

PLANTS *Howea forsteriana*
REGION OF ORIGIN Lord Howe Islands, Pacific Ocean
WILD HABITAT Wet, windy island growing in the undergrowth
HOME HABITAT Shady cool places
COMMON PROBLEMS Few, but gets brown leaves from excessive dryness or *prolonged* waterlogging

---

PLANTS *Hoya carnosa, H. australis*
REGION OF ORIGIN South China, Australia
WILD HABITAT Rainforest, on trees and trailing on ground
HOME HABITAT Bright light in bay window of a living room
COMMON PROBLEMS Stand on a damp pebble tray to increase humidity; does not like disturbance but otherwise easy to grow.

drip profusely with a sticky nectar to attract night pollinators.

The young twining stems of *Hoya carnosa* are covered with reversed hairs which under certain conditions can help to attach the plant to rough and rocky surfaces. The stems of the plant also develop light-avoiding, climbing roots which nestle close to the surface of their support and bond with it, making the stem even more secure. Since the hoya makes itself so secure in this way it does not suffer disturbance well, either through being repotted or having the dead flower buds removed.

The genus is named in honour of Thomas Hoy, who was a gardener for the Duke of Northumberland at Syon House in Middlesex.

Hyacinth

These bulbous plants are temporary house plants, prized for their flowers in winter. They come from the mountainous areas of the east Mediterranean and North Africa and during the winter lie under snow-covered ground, emerging with a head start over most other plants in early spring. So, not surprisingly, they need a cool, dark rooting period over several weeks, and once they flower they need bright light and cool conditions.

When the leaf bud pushes up through the soil it forms a hood made of leaves which prise the soil apart. Once the leaf bud reaches above ground, the outer leaves wither and allow the inner leaves to open out. They stand up obliquely. Their concave upper surfaces are often deeply channelled, so that rain will flow down the grooves towards the centre of the plant into the earth where bulbs and roots are situated.

Hyacinths are very sensitive to temperature, and this is due to their wild ancestry. Warm rooms rapidly kill off the flowers because high temperatures tell the plant that it is summertime, and they go into their resting state. Because the bulbs flower in cool spring mountain air, they enjoy cool rooms in the home, and bedrooms and dining rooms are often a lot better than living rooms.

The strongly scented inflorescence is made up of many flowers which are individually pollinated by insects in the wild. The petals of the flower are often pierced and sucked by flies, bees, and butterflies which can all bore into the flowers.

It has been known for a long time that hyacinths can be grown in water instead of soil, provided they have enough minerals. The idea was popularized by Madame de Pompadour, mistress to Louis XV, who grew 200 hyacinths in glass jars in 1759. These hyacinth glasses became very fashionable in Victorian times when many different designs appeared. How the roots survive completely submerged is a bit of a mystery – most plants which live on land need air in their soil to keep their roots fresh and avoid rotting. However, in the snow melt of spring it is quite likely that the hyacinth roots are well watered. If you look closely at the roots of hyacinth bulbs grown in water you will notice that they have a very 'fuzzy' appearance; this is due to the roots having produced lots more root hairs than they would under normal circumstances in the soil. The root hairs are the absorbing parts of the root and with many more present they can absorb more oxygen as well as water. Even so, bulbs planted in pots can rot, especially in undrained soil when suddenly flooded.

After flowering, the bulbs do not need to be thrown away but will continue to live if kept watered until the bulb withers. The bulb should then be lifted and stored in a cool dry place until replanting in the autumn.

There is only one native species, *Hyacinth orientalis*, which has been much hybridized. The original species is blue or occasionally

---

Hyacinths come from the mountains of the eastern Mediterranean: hot summers, cold winters and springs mean their flowers enjoy cool conditions in the home.

PLANTS *Hyacinth orientalis*
REGION OF ORIGIN East Mediterranean and North Africa
WILD HABITAT Mountainous regions with cold winters
HOME HABITAT Cool dark cupboard for early growth; light moderately cool bedroom for long flowering
COMMON PROBLEMS No flowers or stunted growth when too warm and light in early stages; long leaves if kept in the dark too long; and bulb rot with too much water in soil-filled and undrained containers

white and has fewer and more delicate flowers on a thinner stalk compared to the cultivated type. It is sometimes found growing in rocky crevices which protects it from the grazing of sheep or goats. Hybridization is done by hand pollination, rubbing the stamens of one colour of flower with the stigma of another. One of the reasons that hyacinths are so good to hybridize is that each of the thirty or so flowers on the inflorescence potentially can produce a new variety. The seedlings are planted out after pollination, but it takes five years for a decent-sized bulb to develop.

In the early days of hyacinth growing the bulbs were sold for hundreds of pounds, and rare hybrids were even protected in bird cages! It was probably introduced through the Dutch botanist Carolus Clusius who received a bundle of bulb goodies from the Turk Ogier de Busbecq in 1573. Clusius's bulb garden in Leiden became the source for hyacinth stock and Dutch growers soon exploited the hyacinth potential to produce over 300 varieties by the mid-eighteenth century. In 1753, for example, the catalogue of grower George Voorhelm lists 244 double and 107 single hyacinth varieties, and a hundred years later there were believed to be 2000 sorts. The double-headed variety has gone out of fashion today (there are about six double varieties regularly available), but it has very full beautiful blooms and is well worth

growing. Although there is now a smaller selection of hyacinths available, their popularity is still enormous, and figures for the early 1990s show that 18 million hyacinth plants are sold each year in Holland.

Hydrangea

This group of plants has an almost worldwide distribution in the temperate regions, but the common hydrangea, *Hydrangea macrophylla* (syn. *Hydrangea hortensis*), comes from the southern part of Honshu island, Japan. Here the forest is an open mixture of broadleaved and coniferous trees, and the climate is Mediterranean, with a summer monsoon drenching the plants.

Potted hydrangeas need to be kept cool, at about 10–16°C (50–60°F), and well watered (occasionally soaked) and are best put into the garden or a cool porch after they have flowered. They like a well-lit position as long as they do not get too warm. There are mop-headed (Hortensia) varieties such as *Hydrangea macrophylla* 'Rosita', and lace-capped varieties with flatter flower heads, such as 'Teller'. The mop-headed flowers are mostly all sterile, but the lace-capped ones have fertile flowers surrounded by a ring of much larger petalled sterile ones. Propagation is best done by taking cuttings in early autumn and overwintering them in a garden cold frame.

Curiously the composition of the soil can change the flower colour. For a blue variety to

PLANTS *Hydrangea macrophylla*
REGION OF ORIGIN Honshu island, Japan
WILD HABITAT Bushes growing in open temperate forest
HOME HABITAT Cool but sunny position in porch or hallway, planting outdoors when finished flowering
COMMON PROBLEMS Wilting and death, short flowering if allowed to dry out and kept too warm

be truly blue it needs an acidic compost, and pink varieties need lime.

The first hydrangeas to reach Europe from Japan were probably introduced by Dr Philipp Franz von Siebold, a German doctor and amateur botanist. In 1826 he was working for the Dutch East India Company in Deshima, Japan, but was thrown out two years later for trying to collect Japanese maps, an offence for which he could have been executed. He managed to take his collection of plants, which included mop-headed hydrangeas, back to Holland where he cultivated them in his garden at Ghent.

Hypoestes
[Polka-dot plant]

There are about 40 species of *Hypoestes* from southern Africa and Madagascar. The most commonly cultivated is *Hypoestes phyllostachya* (syn. *Hypoestes sanguinolenta*), a low-growing plant from the tropical rainforests of Madagascar which reaches about 1 m (3 ft) in the wild. It is grown for its pink spotted leaves, although modern varieties can have at least half

Hypoestes phyllostachya

| PLANTS *Hypoestes phyllostachya* |
| REGION OF ORIGIN Madagascar |
| WILD HABITAT Rainforest |
| HOME HABITAT Humid kitchen or bathroom, or living room sitting on damp pebble tray |
| COMMON PROBLEMS Freckling is poor in dull light; with too much water, leaves start to yellow in dry, unmisted conditions |

the leaf surface covered in pink. However, good light encourages the best leaf coloration: olive green leaves with brightly contrasting pink areas. Small violet flowers are produced in summer, and after flowering there is a dormant period for several weeks when watering can be reduced.

In the home they need moderate watering during the growing period and although overwatering won't kill, it causes elongated leaves with spindly growth; so again, to get the best, highly coloured leaves, dryness between waterings is essential. They do need high rainforest humidity with misting and a damp pebble tray beneath the pot.

Polka-dots are greedy plants and should be moved on into larger pots whenever they have filled their pots with roots, as well as being given a twice monthly dose of liquid feed. They tend to get out of control quite quickly, and the growing tips need to be pinched out to keep the plants bushy.

Curiously for rainforest plants the hypoestes can grow in very cool temperatures down to 7°C (45°F) without suffering, and it can survive almost freezing conditions for a short period.

Impatiens wallerana
See Busy Lizzie

Indian rubber plant
See *Ficus elastica*

From left: *Helix ivalace, Hedera helix variegata, H. canariensis, H. helix sagittaefolia*

Ivy
[*Hedera*]

Ivies usually grow in woodlands from Europe to north Africa and Japan. They ramble over the ground in search of rocks and trees to climb up, and use special aerial roots to grasp hold of damp surfaces. Because they often come from temperate climates they are very easy to grow but should not be grown in very warm rooms; suggested temperatures are about 10 – 18°C (50 – 65°F). The indoor ivy is usually a variety of the English ivy, *Hedera helix*, and in the present Dutch plant industry catalogue there are 24 kinds available, from 'Adam' to 'Chicago', 'Hanny' and 'Pittsburgh', but really none are very different from the basic species. However, if indoor varieties were to be put outside they would not survive the winter unless they were planted out in the previous spring and had had a chance to acclimatize and become less 'soft'. Also, indoor varieties are selected for a host of different mutations in leaf shape and variegations, and also for their potential for bushy growth, producing more side shoots than the wild type. These shoots are produced from leaf joints when the main growing stems are 'stopped' by cutting or pinching them out in spring.

The aerial roots of *H. helix* will attach to mossy poles, although this is not necessary for this ivy is just as good as a trailing plant. The other widely available ivy is *Hedera canariensis*, and 'Gloire de Marengo' is the largely yellow and big-leaved variety, but this species has no aerial roots.

As an adaptation to the low light levels in the under-storey of trees, ivy has specially shaped cells in the leaf surface to help reflect light into the working interior of the leaf. They never like direct sunlight but even so they do need to be put close to the windows in winter or else growth will be straggly and variegated types will turn green. In general, anywhere in the house is relatively shaded compared with the outdoors. Watering should be moderate but regular in summer, and more sparing in winter.

With the introduction of central heating, ivy has fallen in the pot plant charts, and they are not the maintenance-free plants they once were. Dry warm rooms lead to scorched crispy leaves and problems can start at temperatures around 16°C (60°F); misting and pebble trays are the cure, as well as moving plants to cool bedrooms and humid bathrooms.

Ivy is a perennial vine with two different types of growth: juvenile and adult. Juvenile branches root readily, adult branches do not. The adult flowers, the juvenile does not. Its juvenile growth habit is that of a creeping vine, but later it becomes shrub-like and forms flowers, and its juvenile leaves have three or five lobes, while adult leaves tend to be entire and rounded. The whole process is probably controlled by chemical triggers or hormones, as it has been shown that by applying artificial hormones the juvenile and adult stages are disrupted. Unless you want your rooms completely overgrown with ivy (and some Victorians did do this) then the indoor ivy in the juvenile stage is the most likely one for you.

Jack-in-the-pulpit
See *Arisaema triphyllum*

PLANTS *Hedera helix*
REGION OF ORIGIN Europe, North Africa and Japan
WILD HABITAT Climbing in the under-storey of trees
HOME HABITAT A light living room away from direct sun, but moving closer to the window in winter, with frequent misting and damp pebble trays in centrally heated homes
COMMON PROBLEMS Brown tips on the leaves when too dry can be cured by misting or relocating in humid bathroom; red spider mite infestation if the air or soil is too dry

---

Jasmine
[*Jasminum*]

One of the jasmines most commonly grown is *Jasminum polyanthum*, the pink jasmine, which comes from the sub-tropical monsoon forest of mid-west China. Winters are mild and summers are hot, and rainfall is very high at over 2.5 m (100 in) per year. *J. polyanthum* can tolerate cool temperatures but dies in frost; it usually thrives in coolish and warm rooms, minimum about 10–15°C (50–59°F), and likes

PLANTS *Jasminum polyanthum,*
J. officinale, etc.
REGION OF ORIGIN Mid-west China
WILD HABITAT Climbing in sub-tropical
monsoon forest
HOME HABITAT On wire frame in
moderately warm dining room or
bedroom
COMMON PROBLEM Drying out in the
summer, leading to rapidly withering and dead
leaves; mist spraying and damp pebble trays are
helpful, but otherwise an easy and rewarding
plant to keep

bright dappled light but not direct sunshine. It
is a very strong climber with winding tendrils
for ever searching out new supports, and in the
home these are usually trained around wire
hoops or cane. The tendrils can grow to 3 m
(9 ft) or more but as soon as vigorous growth
appears in the spring some of the growing
points can be pinched out to keep the plant
bushy, and it needs severe pruning after it has
flowered. *J. polyanthum* flowers in the spring
but another commonly kept species *Jasminum
officinale*, white jasmine, flowers from late
summer to early autumn.

The Chinese jasmines were once thought to
be among the easiest house plants to keep, but
dry air from modern central heating causes the
leaves to die. They are used to humid forest
conditions, so in the home they need regular
misting, and benefit from standing on damp
pebble trays.

Jasmine tea is flavoured with the flowers of
Jasminum sambac, called the Arabian jasmine,
which is sometimes cultivated as 'Maid of
Orleans' or 'Grand Duke of Tuscany' and is
recognized in part by its large leaf size, between
8–13 cm (3–5 in). It comes from India, Burma
and Sri Lanka.

Kalanchoe
[Flaming Katy, Mexican hat plant]

These are small succulent (i.e. fleshy) plants or
shrubs. They come from a wide area of East
Africa including Kenya, Somalia and a part of
Ethiopia, but the most popular come from
southern and central Madagascar where they
grow in bright sun or in the partial shade of
taller shrubs and small trees. In the dry bush
and desert of southern Madagascar, Somalia,
Kenya and Ethiopia they grow on rocks. They
share the same sort of conditions in which cacti
live but, like all succulents, kalanchoes are only
found naturally in Africa so the common name
of *Mexican* hat plant is a bit daft. In the wild
this plant's conservation is not as dire as the
African violet but it is coming close. Yet it is
very easy to grow, requiring little water and very
decorative though some species, such as the
velvet leaf, *Kalanchoe beharensis*, are difficult to
get to flower more than once.

Kalanchoe is a short-day plant – it needs
short day lengths to flower. But it can be
induced to flower out of season by giving bursts
of light during the night. Their natural day
length is about eight hours of light, and
kalanchoes grown like this have small succulent
leaves with smooth edges, whereas plants grown
under long-day conditions with about double
the length of daylight, have large, thin leaves
with notched edges.

Some kalanchoes are very prolific, and the
maternity plant, *Kalanchoe diagremontiana*, gets
its name from the numerous 'babies' (plantlets)
growing in the notches along the leaf margin.
The maternity plant is easily propagated from
these small plants, which in the wild drop to
the soil and take root when they are mature
enough. Other kalanchoes also bear plantlets
round the edges or at the tips of their leaves and
these are dislodged easily by touch. But
Kalanchoe tubiflora has a special catapult device.
The plantlets are produced on a short stalk near
the tip of the cylindrical leaves, and these tiny

Right: *Kalanchoe blossfeldiana*; Left: *K. tormentosa*

plantlets have rounded leaves which form a distinct cup. If a raindrop strikes one this pushes it down; the stalk acts like a springboard and rebounds upwards jerking the plantlet free and throwing it up to 1.5 m (5 ft) away.

Several different types of kalanchoe are grown as house plants. *Kalanchoe blossfeldiana* has striking flowers on tall stems, and breeders are able to produce hybrids which flower all the year round by using the trick of restricting day length. However, it comes from the eastern central region of Madagascar and normally flowers in the spring.

The key to looking after kalanchoes is to keep them moderately cool, at 10°C (50°F) minimum, and bright. Light from an east- or west-facing window in summer is the best, moving them to a south-facing window in winter. They can tolerate cold almost down to freezing, in gritty, well-drained compost, but sparse watering in winter will avoid rot – a basic for most succulents. Sometimes the advice given is to discard the plant after flowering but it can be kept by moving it out of the sun for several weeks and then returning to its original location with a moderate watering. It is true that kalanchoes hardly ever flower with the same profusion the second time round, but with repotting in the spring they can still put on a good show.

PLANTS *Kalanchoe blossfeldiana, K. beharensis*
REGION OF ORIGIN Madagascar and East Africa
WILD HABITAT In scrubland and on rocks
HOME HABITAT Sunny windowsill, south-facing in winter
COMMON PROBLEMS Rotting due to overwatering; elongated stems and misshapen leaves can also be due to overwatering or lack of light; brown spots on the leaves can be due to low humidity and will be helped by misting and standing in a damp pebble tray (not *K. beharensis* from the dry scrub)

Kentia palm
See *Howea forsteriana*

Ladder ferns
See *Nephrolepis*

Lady palm
See *Rhapis excelsa*

Lithops
[Stone plant]

Rarely has a plant defended itself so fantastically as the stone plants. They camouflage themselves as stones in the rocky deserts they live in to avoid being eaten, and the disguise is so convincing it fools a lot of people.

They have two extremely fleshy semi-circular leaves, partially fused along their flattened edge to make a slot in the middle, which is why they're nicknamed 'bum plants'! They come from the arid bushlands of South and South-west Africa and by lying half submerged in sand, gravel or stones they avoid drying out in hot winds and fierce sun. Their thick round leaves are often beautifully mottled in browns, greens and greys so they really do look like

---

Lithops schwantesii

PLANTS *Lithops fulleri,*
L. pseudotruncatella etc.
REGION OF ORIGIN South and South-west
Africa
WILD HABITAT Arid scrubland, and desert,
submerged
HOME HABITAT Full sun of south- or west-
facing window in living room or bedroom
COMMON PROBLEMS Not a very
demanding plant, they rot if overwatered
but thrive on neglect except in spring and
early summer when they need moderate
watering

stones. In fact, the disguise is so good they are
very difficult to find in the wild except for the
couple of weeks during the wet season when a
large daisy-like flower appears between the two
fleshy leaves. But even then, there are so many
other plants in flower at the same time that the
Lithops can afford the risk of revealing itself.

Coming from deserts it needs the best,
bright light available, on a south- or west-facing
window at about 10–18°C (50–65°F) although
much colder temperatures can be tolerated. To
mimic the desert-like conditions of the dry
season, between October and March, there
should be no water at all. It is important for
flowering that they go through this shrivelled
dry stage before the first spring watering, when
they swell up and look happy. Spring also
brings the light they need to grow after this
dormant phase, when the old pair of leaves
separate and a new pair pushes through. During
spring and early summer they need watering
when the surface becomes dry. But watering
should be stopped again after June, with a final
wetting in early autumn just before the flowers
appear.

Although the surface of *Lithops* lies almost
flush with the ground it has a clever 'fibre optic'
system to pass light down to the green
photosynthesizing cells below. The light enters
through translucent windows at the top of the
leaves and down a clear jelly-filled tube to the
green tissue below the soil.

The seeds of the stone plant are dispersed by
rain, and some species contain an air pocket
which allows them to float for several days,
often in violent and torrential rain downpours
and floods in the desert.

Lithops was discovered by the English
explorer William Burchell in 1811: 'On picking
up from the stony ground, what was supposed
to be a curiously shaped pebble, it proved to be
a plant.'

Maidenhair fern

[*Adiantum*]

See also FERNS

This is one of the most popular house plants
and comes from tropical Latin America. It
grows in humid forest under-storeys, rocky sites
and streams with flecks of light piercing
through. Because it is adapted to wet conditions
it must never be allowed to dry out in the
home, and needs a good soaking. It often grows
on moss-covered rocks or fallen trees on the
floors of the humid forests, so as a house plant
it needs a moist yet free-draining rooting
mixture, with grit and crocking of terracotta at
the bottom to prevent it getting sodden.

This is a big genus with a wide choice of
species of varying sizes and shaped fronds. The
bigger ones tend to be tropical and should not
be kept lower than 15°C (60°F), e.g. varieties
such as 'Brilliantelse', 'Fragrans' and
'Monocolor'. They all need to be kept in high
humidity, for example by misting with a spray.
But they do much better in a conservatory or

PLANTS *Adiantum*
REGION OF ORIGIN Tropical Latin
America
WILD HABITAT Under-storeys of rainforests
HOME HABITAT Kitchens, bathrooms in
warm, humid shady spots
COMMON PROBLEMS Lack of water and
humidity kills the leaves; draughts are fatal

The delicate leaves of maidenhair ferns are adapted to the dappled sunlight on tropical woodland floors and make an exquisite foliage house plant.

terrarium than a house because they don't like dry rooms.

The good side is that they are well adapted to low light conditions, and make excellent plants for the more humid and shadier rooms, such as bathrooms and kitchens. But they do need to be kept warm, and draughts must be avoided.

Mammillaria

See also Cacti

Mammillaria are round, ball-shaped cacti distributed throughout the south-west USA, Mexico and Central America. It is one of the most popular of all cactus genera. The number

> **PLANTS** *Mammillaria*
> **REGION OF ORIGIN** South-west USA,
> Mexico and Central America
> **WILD HABITAT** Deserts and scrubland
> **HOME HABITAT** Sunny windowsills
> **COMMON PROBLEMS** Too much watering
> during the rest period in winter

Maranta leuconeura 'Erythrophylla'

of spines varies greatly: *Mammillaria plumosa* is completely obscured by feathery spines but others, such as *Mammillaria sheldonii*, bear long hooked spines. The woolly hairs of *Mammillaria* are a sunscreen to block the glaring hot sun of its native drylands, and many species naturally grow in arid grassland, protected from the worst of the sun's rays. In the home the light is many times less than the natural intensity and so *Mammillaria* will grow quite happily on sunny windowsills.

The majority of species flower easily even as small plants, most having small white, red or pink flowers produced in a ring around the upper part of the plant in early summer.

The most commonly available species are grown in well-drained compost and need plenty of watering in the growing season but cut to almost nothing in winter between about November and March. Even so, when grown in a warm, dry, centrally heated house they will need light watering just once or twice in the winter. Plants should be kept cool in this almost dry state until the flower buds appear in late spring.

Maranta

[Prayer plant]

Marantas are low-growing creeping plants from the rainforests of Brazil, usually found in clearings where the sun partially penetrates the hot, humid forest. Since it is a rainforest plant it needs a moist atmosphere, but with its shallow rooting it is good for hanging baskets. Marantas enjoy generous watering during the

summer, and misting is a good idea in dry centrally heated conditions.

The colourful red-veined variety *Maranta tricolor* (syn. *Maranta leuconeura erythrophylla*) is the most popular, but the basic species, *Maranta leuconeura massangeana*, has very elegant silvery white veins and is worth growing.

One interesting behaviour of the marantas, and the reason for their other name of 'prayer plants', is that their leaves follow the sun during the day, and at night they fold and raise their leaves together and then unfold them again at dawn. By moving the leaves during the day they scavenge more flecks of light on the forest floor. However, prolonged direct sunlight can be

> **PLANTS** *Maranta*
> **REGION OF ORIGIN** Tropical Latin
> America
> **WILD HABITAT** Hot, humid forest floors
> **HOME HABITAT** Half-shaded, humid places,
> bathroom, hallways
> **COMMON PROBLEM** Lack of humidity dries
> out the leaves to produce dead edges, and they
> need regular misting with water

harmful, and the house plants need half-shade out of the sun.

It's difficult to explain why many marantas have red veins. In some cases red coloured leaves may protect the chlorophyll from bleaching in the sun. But the regular patternings and vein-colourings are harder to explain. It has been suggested that they act as attractions to insects in order to pollinate the rather insignificant little flowers, but there are plenty of plants with equally small flowers and plain green leaves. Such colouring is not to be confused with variegation, which is usually due to chloroplast mutation and seldom persists in the wild.

Incidentally, these species are related to the arrowroot plant, from which arrowroot is obtained from the rhizomes.

Microcoelum
[Dwarf coconut palm]

See also PALMS

Dwarf coconut palms, of which there are only two species, grow in the mountainous tropical forests of eastern Brazil with daily rain and therefore air saturated with moisture, and shady conditions. *Microcoelum weddelianum* (syn. *Cocos weddeliana*) is the cultivated species and is a small palm even in its native environment, growing to 1.5 m (5 ft) tall and 3 cm (1 in) in trunk diameter, so it never reaches the full sun of the forest canopy.

In the home they should never be put in direct sun or in very dry places such as next to radiators, otherwise brown leaf tips develop. Even though they thrive on warmth, minimum 18°C (65°F), dwarf coconut palms need very moist air, so mist spraying, a moist tray to stand on, or being grouped with other moisture-loving plants is practically essential. They should receive thorough watering but should dry out a little before repeating. If you have a conservatory or a warm greenhouse it is possible to treat this rather fussy palm as a temporary

---

> **PLANTS** *Microcoelum weddelianum*
> **REGION OF ORIGIN** Brazil
> **WILD HABITAT** Rainforests
> **HOME HABITAT** Can survive living rooms
> **COMMON PROBLEMS** Leaf tips turn brown in dry hot air or when compost is allowed to dry out completely

resident in the house, bringing it in to the drier environment for up to two years before a recovery period under glass.

Miltonia
[Pansy orchid]

See also ORCHIDS

These are tropical orchids from Brazil and Colombia, with pansy-like flowers. The plants perch up in trees without touching the ground and this gives them access to daylight but presents all sorts of other problems. They suffer sporadic shortages of water, and have a meagre diet of small bits of humus caught in the tree's bark, as well as minerals washed down the tree trunk in the rain. So as house plants, miltonias don't need much in the way of nutrition; they need open, airy, well-drained and poor soil which can be provided by using a high proportion of inert material such as vermiculite in the compost.

They also have a swollen stem to hold a reservoir of water to see them through the short droughts. But they do rely on humidity to keep

---

> **PLANTS** *Miltonia*
> **REGION OF ORIGIN** Colombia and Brazil
> **WILD HABITAT** Perched on trees
> **HOME HABITAT** Bright living room in winter with plenty of humidity through misting and pebble tray; cooler bedroom in summer
> **COMMON PROBLEMS** Lack of humidity can be fatal

their leaves fresh and cut down water losses from the leaves, and regular misting, damp pebble trays, or a generally humid room, are essential.

Coming from a hot climate, miltonias also need warmth during the winter, minimum temperature 18°C (65°F), and if they are kept humid enough, can grow in a bright living room and come into flower. But they are seasonal plants, and in summer they need to be kept fairly cool during their rest period, so they should be moved to a cooler bedroom, for example.

Mimosa pudica
[Sensitive plant]

Mimosa grows in sunny hot climates throughout the tropics where it thrives as a rambling shrub, and even as a 'weed' in tropical grass lawns. The fascination for growing it at home is its astonishing animal-like behaviour when its feathery leaves instantly fold on being touched or wounded. This behaviour may confuse grazing animals as the plant appears to almost 'vanish' when any attempt is made to eat it – not to mention the battery of sharp thorns which are exposed on the stem. It can also avoid being battered by tropical downpours.

The leaves recover from touching after several minutes or more, depending on the surrounding air temperature and how hard the leaves have been hit. But if you want to be exceptionally cruel, the most dramatic movements are made when you start to cut or burn the leaves, and you can watch the pairs of leaflets fold up in sequence, like a chain reaction of collapsing deckchairs, until the whole leaf stalk collapses.

The stem can grow weak and straggly and often needs supporting because the plant has a naturally rambling, rather than an upright growth. In summer it produces purple or pink flowers which look like small fluffy balls.

The plant really appreciates humidity,

PLANTS *Mimosa pudica*
REGION OF ORIGIN Tropical Americas, but widespread throughout the tropics
WILD HABITAT A small rainforest shrub
HOME HABITAT Bright sunny windowsills with humidity, e.g. in kitchen
COMMON PROBLEM Not enough heat or light makes the leaves sluggish at moving and in extreme shade the leaves fall off

---

warmth, at about 20°C (68°F), water when its soil looks dry and bright sunny positions. In winter it suffers so badly from the poor quality and quantity of daylight that its leaves fall off, which is a very unnatural thing for it to do in the wild. The only remedy is to use artificial lights, such as special plant grow-bulbs available from electrical shops, or simply to throw the plant away and regrow it from seed the following spring.

The plant is very easy to grow from seed, which can be sown in ordinary potting compost in a warm place and a plastic bag tied over the top to make it humid, recreating the ground conditions in the tropics.

Mosaic plant
See *Fittonia*

Monstera deliciosa
See Swiss cheese plant

Moth orchid
See *Phalaenopsis*

Mother-in-law's tongue
See *Sansevieria trifasciata*

Mother-of-thousands
See *Saxifraga stolonifera*

Narcissus
See Daffodil

Neoregelia
[Blushing bromeliad]

See also BROMELIADS

Neoregelias are widespread in the tropical rainforests of Brazil, where they tend to grow on the lower parts of trees, moderately shaded. They are mostly grown for their bright glossy leaf rosettes, red in the centre and green towards the outside. Their flowers bloom in the cup of water at the centre of the rosette, but they are small and insignificant. However, once the house plant has flowered the whole rosette dies and the only way of prolonging its life once in flower is to keep it cool and shaded. The minimum temperature for neoregelias is 10°C (50°F). When the rosette has started to decay, new plantlets at the base of the plant can be broken off and propagated, provided they have already started to grow their own roots. After two or three years the new plants should come into flower.

Normally these bromeliads need moderately bright light, because although slightly shaded in the forest, the light in the home is not nearly as intense as that of the Brazilian tropics. However, direct sunlight is not good for these bromeliads.

Since *Neoregelia* lives in very humid rainforest and in humid coastal forest as well, the house plant needs a regular misting with water. Tepid rain-water needs to be used for general watering to avoid cold shock and the lime from hard tap-water. The 'vase' between the leaf bases should occasionally be filled with water but the roots of *Neoregelia* are not very

---

PLANTS *Neoregelia*
REGION OF ORIGIN Brazil
WILD HABITAT Lower trunks of trees
HOME HABITAT Bathrooms, kitchens and other warm, humid places
COMMON PROBLEMS Overwatering and overfilling central cup causes rot

---

well developed and are susceptible to overwatering. 'Flandria' and 'Perfecta Tricolor' are variegated, being green and cream with a central red rosette and have small blue flowers in the central vase. Only water to the base of these flowers as overfilling will cause rot.

When the plant approaches flowering time, the leaf bases around the cup in the middle turn a brilliant scarlet which attracts hummingbirds in the wild.

Nephrolepis
[Ladder ferns]

See also FERNS

These occur worldwide all over the tropics in a wide temperature range, 9°C (48°F) for the coolest species, but the more tropical species only go down to 16°C (60°F). Two main species are cultivated, *Nephrolepis cordifolia* from the woodlands of West Indies and Chile and *Nephrolepis exaltata*, which has a huge number of naturally occurring varieties in regions such as Australia, Florida, Brazil, Africa, and Southeast Asia. Correspondingly there are many cultivated varieties of *N. exaltata* such as 'Atlanta' (delicate pointed fronds), 'Bostoniensis' (dark green) and 'Teddy Junior' (small fronds).

Ladder ferns are weedy species in the tropics and grow anywhere on disturbed land, for example building sites, volcanic lava, erosion and hurricane damaged sites. These are open places with very little competition from other plants and they quickly complete their life cycles by producing rapidly growing spores.

Unusually, in comparison with many ferns, *Nephrolepis* species are adapted to dry sunny conditions so live well as house plants and can tolerate dry house conditions and good sun, if they are standing in damp pebble trays. They do best in the more humid conditions of sunny kitchens and bathrooms. They were very popular in Victorian times and are now undergoing another revival.

PLANTS *Nephrolepis*
REGION OF ORIGIN Mainly tropical, worldwide
WILD HABITAT Ground living
HOME HABITAT Especially happy in kitchens and bathrooms
COMMON PROBLEMS Lack of humidity stunts growth by making fronds die back; lack of light causes straggly fronds

Prolonged sun can be a problem for these ferns and very dry conditions make all the frond segments drop off to cut down water losses, which could be a useful adaptation in the wild in exposed places. If the segments do fall off it permanently damages the fronds, although the plant recovers by growing new fronds from the base. However, some dropping of the segments is normal.

Another interesting adaptation is that they are one of the very few ferns to have stolons – runners like strawberry plants which send small plantlets out to colonize the ground around them. Only one or two plants will colonize a whole lava field, although the plant has to be mature to send out runners. It does this in cultivation but less so in a house – more so in a conservatory – and the stolons spread out, producing new plants which can be cut off and cultivated.

ORCHIDS

Most tropical orchids are epiphytes, clinging to the sides of trees for support. This is a clever adaptation on their part to avoid the shade of the forest floor, while staying in sunlight without having to go to the expense of growing a large woody trunk like a tree in order to reach the light. But it is a precarious existence with shortages of water and nutrients.

Epiphytic orchids have become specialized to a life without soil. They have extensive systems of aerial roots to absorb moisture and dissolved nutrients and have either developed storage

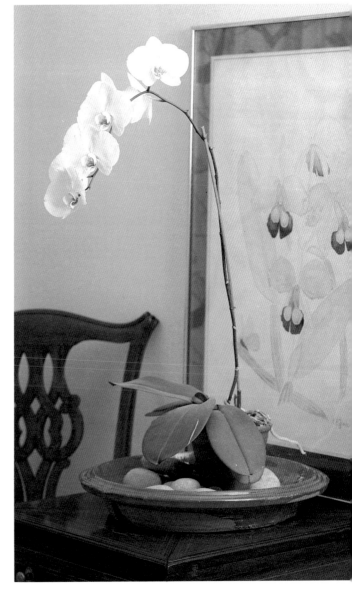

Dendrobium bigibbum

organs called 'pseudobulbs' or have thick fleshy leaves to store water.

The roots of orchids have a fantastic variety of structures that is worth mentioning in detail. There are thick, rigid roots specially adapted for anchoring the plant to its support, and they in turn are covered in a fur of 'root hairs' alongside the tree's bark. When the tip of one of these root hairs touches the bark it grows firm, using so called 'absorption' cells. Once fixed, the roots flatten out and they can absorb minerals and water from the compost of decaying vegetable matter trapped in the craggy bark.

But some roots also dangle in the air for no apparent reason. These thick, sometimes green or silvery roots have a special structure. The covering skin (epidermis) is made up of several layers of cells called the 'velamen' which protects the inner core of the root as well as preventing it from losing too much water. The spongy quality of the root may also help it

Orchids included in this book:
Cymbidium   Dendrobium
Phalaenopsis Miltonia

absorb moisture from the damp air, and in some species it can also photosynthesize like a leaf. The velamen can also absorb rain-water directly as moisture trickling down the bark, which is likely to contain minerals from decaying leaves and other humus. The velamen becomes full of water after rain but in dry weather contains air pockets and acts as an insulating layer against excessive heating as well as loss of water.

The tree's bark can often dry out rapidly even after a torrential downpour, but silt from debris collected under the centre of the plant and sometimes around the roots, keep it mulched with moisture. Epiphytic mosses on the trunk often provide another reservoir of water.

Because the roots photosynthesize they need a supply of carbon dioxide. In leaves this gas is 'breathed' in through leaf pores called stomata, which open and close like small mouths according to the time of day, moisture, light, and so on. The epiphytic orchid roots have their own types of opening and closing pores too, but they only respond to moisture, opening during humid times and pinching shut to save water in dry conditions.

All these adaptations are important methods of surviving the dry seasons when there is less rain. But what does it all mean for the cultivation of orchids?

For successful cultivation, it is essential to provide a bright, buoyant atmosphere, watering them only occasionally but regularly misting their leaves and roots with fresh rain-water.

Good drainage is essential or else rot will set in, and sometimes you need to enlarge the drainage holes in the flower pots they are grown in. Chips of bark or fibrous peat, grit, perlite or perlag, fragments of expanded polystyrene and

Phalaenopsis amabilis

pieces of charcoal mixed with chopped sphagnum or shredded leaves can all be used to mix into the compost. When the pots are filled the bottom third should contain crocks or large stones, with the rest filled up with the loose compost. Some growers just use inert materials such as vermiculite for the whole compost and have great success.

The more natural tree conditions can be mimicked in the home too. Baskets made of cork-oak bark are ideal for plants which need to dry out thoroughly between watering. Trimmed slabs of cork-oak bark or prepared tree fern fibre make a suitable mounting surface for all epiphytes.

Orchids are used to very poor nutrition when they are hanging on to the sides of trees. Most of their nutrition is from rain-water trickling down through humus on the tree's trunk and branches, a bit of decaying mulch around the leaf bases, or any minerals floating in the forest mist. Because of their poor compost, most orchids appreciate extra fertilizer during the growing season, and a half-strength liquid feed in their water is absorbed by the plants very easily.

Rain-water is best for watering, preferably at room temperature during the morning on sunny days so that the plants will dry out while the temperatures are rising; they also appreciate being misted to help delay drying out. Watering once a fortnight is sufficient in winter. They will flourish in summer temperatures of 15–18°C (60–65°F) and winter temperatures ranging from 10–13°C (50–55°F).

PALMS

Palms are among the most successful plants on earth, with over 2000 species growing over a wide range of terrain and climate. However, although the average picture of a marooned mariner shows a desert island with a palm in the middle, the palm – as well as the mariner – are a bit of a myth. Most domestic palms such as parlour palms, don't like direct sunlight but coming originally from the forest under-storey, they need partial shade. They hate being overwatered, so they need to be well drained. Putting broken bits of terracotta or gravel under the soil in their pot will help, but in the spring and summer watering more thoroughly won't hurt. Palms prefer a restricted pot and detest root movement. Even respectful handling will seriously check growth.

The Dutch, with their exploitation of the East Indies in the eighteenth century, were probably the first to bring cane and feather palms to Europe. An honourable mention should be made of the pioneering Dutch botanist and merchant Georg Eberhard Rumpf, who made a study of the flora of the Moluccas in the mid-seventeenth century, and first illustrated many different species of palm. He was also, however, the unluckiest man in the world, growing blind, losing his family in an earthquake, and having his life's work burnt in a fire. It wasn't until forty years after his death that his reworked *Herbarium Amboinense*, a six-volume flora, was published. After his death in 1702 his grave was dug up by a party of English soldiers looking for gold; it was replaced by a second monument to honour his name, but this too was destroyed by a bomb in the Second World War.

In Britain the Victorian fashion for palms was fuelled by glass stovehouses, epitomized by the magnificent palm house at Kew Gardens built in 1848, with 9000 sq.m. (45,000 sq.ft) of glass. Palms portrayed the nineteenth-century vision of perfection, a touch of paradise in the parlour. Added to this the palm proved to be a

---

PALMS included in this book:

Chrysalidocarpus
Date palms (*Phoenix*)
Howea forsteriana (kentia palm)
Microcoelum weddellianum
Parlour palm (*Chamaedorea elegans*)
Rhapis excelsa (lady palm)

tenacious and hardy house plant and for the Victorians this held the position that *Ficus benjamina* enjoys today.

Going back into geological history the palms are older than the flowering plants, dating back 120 million years.

Pansy orchid

See *Miltonia*

Parlour palm

[*Chamaedorea elegans*]

See also PALMS

These palms are found in the undergrowth of lowland tropical forests of relatively dry soils and on limestone in Mexico and Guatemala, and it is adapted to grow like a forest tree. *Chamaedorea* shares many of the characteristics of the kentia palm. It needs heat and it is very tolerant of dry central heating, very low light, overwatering or underwatering and neglect in general. It will flourish, however, if given a damp pebble tray and kept in moderately bright but never full sunlight. The minimum winter temperature should not fall below 10°C (50°F).

The parlour palm has a bamboo-like edible stem with a coloured top to deter predators from eating it. It is a dioecious plant, i.e. produces separate male and female plants, which helps ensure cross-fertilization. Even though it is a popular house plant, it is now vulnerable in the wild.

PLANTS *Chamaedorea elegans*
REGION OF ORIGIN Mexico, Guatemala
WILD HABITAT Dry limestone soil under rainforest trees
HOME HABITAT Practically anywhere, but won't survive total darkness
COMMON PROBLEMS Red spider mites are a problem in hot dry rooms, and can be curbed by regular misting

---

Passiflora caerulea

[Passion flower]

A very vigorous climber from the jungles of South America. It adapts well to life indoors and is a hardy type, but needs humidity measures in dry rooms, with a damp pebble tray and misting. Since it is a vigorously growing plant it needs plenty of water in the summer and twice monthly feeds with a standard liquid fertilizer. It also enjoys good light from a south-facing window. The plant can be trained up wire hoops, canes and even room dividers. The tendrils of the plant are very fast and start coiling within about a minute of touching a suitable surface.

Passiflora has beautiful blue, green and white filaments to its flower, and these probably gave

---

Passiflora caerulea

PLANTS *Passiflora caerulea*
REGION OF ORIGIN Brazil
WILD HABITAT Climber in rainforest
HOME HABITAT In warm room stood in a
moist pebble tray
COMMON PROBLEM Flower buds fall if not
kept humid

rise to its name. The Latin *passio* is part of the
verb to suffer, and it is thought that Jesuit
missionaries in South America gave it this name
to represent the 'Passion of Christ' which they
saw in the flower. The crossed central stigma
was said to represent the three nails with which
Jesus was nailed to the cross and many of the
other parts of the flower were given a symbolic
biblical reference.

Peace lily

See AROIDS

Pelargonium

[Geraniums]

Pelargoniums have been so thoroughly bred
into hybrids that it is sometimes difficult to
know which species they originally came from,
but they all originate from South Africa, most
species growing in dry shrubby bushlands.

Pelargoniums grow on sandy, well-drained
soil, with very poor nutrients. Some have
underground tubers, or succulent stems in
order to store water and withstand drought.
The biggest problem in looking after
pelargoniums is overwatering them. They
should be allowed to dry out a little between
watering and kept almost dry in winter.
Coming from exposed, sunny habitats they
enjoy good direct light so they make excellent
windowsill plants even for south-facing
windows.

The commonest types are the so-called zonal
pelargoniums, and they are recognized by the
purple 'horse-shoe' brand on their leaves.
Pelargonium zonale is the original wild species,

Pelargonium peltatum 'Jeanne d'Arc'

growing in an area between Tulbagh to George
in the south-western Cape of South Africa.
Zonal perlargoniums are scrambling plants
supported on other plants or growing through
other vegetation. They have succulent stems for
withstanding long periods of drought, but they
cannot tolerate frost because they do not
experience it in the wild. They prefer warm to
cool temperatures though ideally not below

PLANTS *Pelargonium* (geraniums)
REGION OF ORIGIN South Africa
WILD HABITAT Sandy, well-drained soil
HOME HABITAT Living rooms with some
direct sunlight
COMMON PROBLEMS Yellow crisp leaves
from underwatering, spindly growth in too
little light

In hanging basket: *Pelargonium capitatum*

10°C (50°F) in winter, although they have been known to tolerate down to about 3°C (38°F). You can keep them all the year round if you take cuttings and keep them warm, but they flower throughout late spring and summer.

Pelargonium peltatum (ivy-leafed geranium) has a particularly weak stem and scrambles over the ground which is why it makes an excellent trailing house plant. It is like the zonal pelargoniums, but not quite as drought tolerant because its stem is not as thick. As it is often used in hanging baskets it tends to dry out more quickly, and needs careful watering. *P. peltatum* comes from the eastern districts of the Cape and flowers in early summer.

Pelargonium tongaense is from north-east Natal, for a pelargonium, comes from a very strange habitat: lowland, quite moist woodland, quite tropical and not subject to long periods of drought or intense sunlight. So as a house plant it does well in shady areas and requires misting in very dry rooms.

Regal pelargoniums are woody shrubs derived largely from *Pelargonium sectional* and *Pelargonium grandiflorum*. The regals are fussy about flowering, and need 12 hours of daylight each day to flower just for a short period, so in Europe they come into flower during early summer. In winter they need only very light watering.

Scented pelargoniums have amazingly aromatic leaves, and there are varieties with subtly different smells varying from lemony to apple-like. The fragrance could well be an anti-herbivore device. Some are woody shrubs and some are much more delicate and have small underground tubers to withstand drought.

Peperomia
[Pepper elder]

These plants inhabit the humid tropical rainforests of West Indies and Latin America. So they do like air humidity and should be stood in damp pebble trays and misted. Their

---

PLANTS *Peperomia*
REGION OF ORIGIN West Indies and Latin America
WILD HABITAT In rainforest, scrabbling over tree trunks and rocks
HOME HABITAT In moderate light e.g. kitchen, with damp pebble tray
COMMON PROBLEMS Rot from overwatering and too much soil; death from low temperatures

---

upright flower spikes, like little candles, are an attractive feature.

The pepper elder has a multiple layered thick skin (epidermis) for storing water in the leaf, as well as creeping stems for exploiting large areas. Many are naturally epiphytic, scrambling over tree trunks and rocks in the tropics, so they are not used to growing in deep soil and do not have very well developed root systems. So they must not be overwatered: in fact they need very careful watering, allowing the compost to begin to dry out sufficiently to let air into the soil before watering again. Since peperomias grow with practically no soil around their roots and have a shallow root system they need just a small pot filled with well-drained compost.

They cannot tolerate temperatures below 10°C (50°F) unless they are fairly dry at the root. They need moderately bright light, about 2 m (6 ft) from a window, and warm temperatures.

Phalaenopsis
[Moth orchid]

See also ORCHIDS

They naturally grow in tropical forests clinging to the bark of trees with their fleshy epiphytic roots and they need a special orchid compost made of bark. They often send roots up over the surface of the compost and edge of the pot as if they are trying to escape. They are best hung from moss-filled baskets or attached to

PLANTS *Phalaenopsis*
REGION OF ORIGIN   South-east Asia and
Australia
WILD HABITAT   Epiphytes of tropical forests,
growing with roots exposed
HOME HABITAT   Bright light, but not
constant direct sunlight
COMMON PROBLEMS   Limpness due to lack
of light; mouldy leaves and roots which are not
well ventilated enough; repotting during
flowering will abort the flowers

moss-covered bark to allow air around the roots. To flower, they need good light perhaps with a few hours direct light, although the light from a south- or west-facing window might scorch the leaves. But good light is so important that it can be worthwhile moving the plants closer to windows, though not draughty ones, during the winter; otherwise, supplement with artificial light. They need temperatures of 18–21°C (65–70°F), with high humidity. Lower temperatures can be tolerated but the plants are not so likely to grow well and flower. Having said that, it is one of the best orchids for flowering in the home.

The first moth orchid was probably recorded by Georg Eberhard Rumpf on the island of Amboina in the mid-seventeenth century.

Philodendron

See also AROIDS

There are two types of *Philodendron*: climbers and non-climbers.

PLANTS *Philodendron*
REGION OF ORIGIN   Latin America
WILD HABITAT   Tropical rainforest
HOME HABITAT   Living room, kept humid
in moderate shade, not too far from a window
COMMON PROBLEMS   Generally hardy,
but do not put in direct sunlight or a
very dry room

Climbers such as *Philodendron elegans* start life growing on forest floors in search of trees and on finding a tree trunk, produce special grappling roots to climb up the tree in search of light. They then drop special 'foraging' roots to the forest floor to hunt for more trees to climb. This is why you need to support the stems with mossy poles when growing climbing philodendrons as house plants.

In contrast, non-climbing philodendrons, such as *Philodendron bipinnatifidum*, perch high up in treetops, germinating in patches of humus on the branches, and are able to support their stems themselves.

Most philodendrons adapt well to indoors, especially if given plenty of humidity. Good light is needed for close, bunched-up growth, as if the plants were in the tops of the trees in the jungle. But in poor light they grow straggly and elongated as if they are on a forest floor. They need temperatures between 15–20°C (59–68°F), and although lower temperatures are tolerated they don't grow much under 10°C (50°F). They also appreciate being watered with tepid water to avoid getting their roots cold.

There are many species and varieties of *Philodendron*. Of the climbing types, *Philodendron angustisectum* has amazing feathery leaves, and the commonest one, *Philodendron scandens*, has heart-shaped leaves. The climbing philodendrons need their stems supported but if left without a support they also make good trailing plants, and being able to tolerate shade they will be suitable for bathrooms where there is some daylight and humidity. The non-climbers grow larger, and the more common *P. bipinnatifidum* has a manageable growing size of about 1 m (3 ft) tall when mature. *Philodendron* is well named because translated literally it means 'love of trees'.

Phoenix

See Date palms

Phyllitis scolopendrium

See Hart's tongue fern

Pilea cadierei

Pilea cadierei

[Aluminium plant]

Generally a low-growing, creeping-stemmed herb. The *Pilea* genus is widespread in the tropical Americas and south-east Asia, but the peculiar thing is that this species, *Pilea cadierei*, has only once been found in the wild, in Vietnam; all the plants in cultivation derive from that one plant.

PLANTS *Pilea cadierei*
REGION OF ORIGIN Vietnam
WILD HABITAT Low-growing herb in open tropical forest
HOME HABITAT Windowsills but not in direct sunlight
COMMON PROBLEMS Rot through overwatering especially in winter

---

Aluminium plants are not too much trouble to look after and make good plants for the windowsill. They need good, but not direct, sunlight such as that provided in east- and west-facing windows. Never leave water in a saucer beneath the pot. The plants can get a bit straggly and need cutting to keep it down. They need pruning after six months to a year to keep them looking neat.

The deep green leaves are marked with fantastic silver blotches caused by air spaces between the cuticle and the centre of the leaf. The air spaces probably behave like mirrors, helping to reflect and scatter light inside the leaf to illuminate the chloroplasts – another adaptation to living in shady conditions.

Pineapple

See *Ananas comosus*

Pinguicula

See Butterworts

Platycerium

See Stag's horn fern

Poinsettia

[*Euphorbia pulcherrima*]

See also *Euphorbia*

Flowers attract their insect visitors by all sorts of means – colour, scent, texture, and so on. The most obvious is by becoming glamorous – large, showy, bright, and colourful. But the flowers of Poinsettia are small and greenish and are not very attractive. Instead, they use bright red floral leaves (bracts) around the flowers to attract hummingbirds to the flowers.

The poinsettia grows in wet, wooded ravines and on rocky hillsides in Mexico, and although it needs only moderately warm conditions it hates draughts. The naturally short day length makes it flower, and during the European summer the house plant needs to be covered for

Euphorbia pulcherrima

PLANTS *Euphorbia pulcherrima*
REGION OF ORIGIN Mexico
WILD HABITAT Arid and sunny scrubland
HOME HABITAT Near a bright window in warm room
COMMON PROBLEMS Loss of leaves due to overwatering; if flower heads fall off, and the leaves turn brown in excessively dry rooms, then they need misting

produce new leaf growth and flowers. In the wild this drying out probably corresponds to the dry rest season.

Keep out of the reach of young children and animals because the leaves are poisonous and cause nausea, vomiting and a burning sensation of the mouth. The poison is deadly for dogs, in particular.

Polka-dot plant
See *Hypoestes*

Polypodium aureum
See Hare's foot fern

Pot rose
[*Rosa chinensis minima*]

'If the Rose is a suitable plant for pot-culture, it will undoubtedly continue to gain friends, if not, no praise of ours can essentially serve it.' That was written in 1848 by William Paul in his

part of the day. Ideally it should have about 14 hours of darkness every day for eight weeks for the best floral bracts to form. Commercial growers cover the plants for three weeks at high temperatures. Poinsettias need a lot of warmth for flowering; 22°C (72°F) which leads to fast growth, but as flowering begins the temperature should be reduced to about 19–20°C (64–68°F) to expand bract size. This temperature treatment is replacing an older, chemical treatment, and it also gives lush growth and short size. The house plant should be kept in a warm room, with reasonable light, for example on a living room table near a window.

It is happy in centrally heated rooms, prefers a dry compost surface between watering and sometimes can even tolerate drying out. After flowering it is often discarded but you can save it by keeping it almost dry, and pruning the plant stem back to the stump. The pot needs to be kept in a shady but moderately warm position until May when rewatering will

PLANTS *Rosa chinensis minima*
REGION OF ORIGIN Probably China
WILD HABITAT Probably from open deciduous forest
HOME HABITAT Well-lit rooms; treat as a temporary plant to return outdoors after flowering
COMMON PROBLEMS Warm and dry rooms cause wilting and flower drop; stand in pebble tray or move to cooler room

classic, *The Rose Garden*, so it seems safe to say that the potted rose did continue to gain friends, as they are now among the most valuable pot plant sales in the UK.

China not tea roses are the best, although you should be aware that the China rose is considered by some to be more plebeian, and that the tea rose has a certain snob value but is more difficult to grow indoors!

The China rose in question is of course not a large bush but a miniature: *Rosa chinensis minima*, or hybrids thereof such as 'Baby Darling' and 'Angela Rippon'.

Vigorous bloomers these, known to the Victorians sometimes as 'Monthly Roses', and flowering indoors from early spring to late summer. Their recipe for keeping indoor roses was to transfer them from the garden in autumn, rest them in a cellar during the winter, prune vigorously and put the roses in a well-lit

room in the spring for early flowering. In late summer they were returned again to the garden. Easy really – they were just treating it as an outdoor plant which is brought indoors for flowering. Indoors it needs maximum light, lots of water and a cool, airy room with a temperature of around 10°C (50°F). In the late summer/autumn it can be repotted and the pot itself sunk into the soil of an outdoor bed.

R. chinensis minima is very close to *Rosa rouletti*, discovered by Dr Roulette from Switzerland. Although it is not certain how it came to be in Switzerland *R. rouletti* is similar to an old European rose called Pompon de Paris from the eighteenth century. This in turn was probably brought from Persia at an even earlier period via a trade caravan from China.

Of course, *R. chinensis minima* is ultimately related to all other roses, which have a fossil lineage millions of years old. But the truth is no one really knows where roses come from as they are found in countries from Greenland to China, Mexico to Siberia. It is interesting, though, that none was found as a native of the southern hemisphere.

Prayer plant

See *Maranta*

Primula

There are over 500 species in the genus which come from all over the world, though mainly in the temperate northern hemisphere from China to Britain. As far as growing them indoors goes, they can be split into two groups: hardy ones which should be placed in the garden again after flowering, and more tender species which are full-time plants for the house and conservatory.

Primula acaulis, also known as *Primula vulgaris*, is a native of Britain. Cultivated forms, including doubles, started to appear in the sixteenth century and were known on the continent as 'English flowers'. The large

Rosa chinensis minima

number of hybrids produced in this country was attributed to our moist and mild climate which allowed gardeners to transplant, trim and manipulate the primroses all through the year.

Colours other than the cream and yellow were unknown until the early part of the seventeenth century when a red or purple variety, *Primula acaulis rubra* (syn. *Primula sibthorpii*), was brought in from Greece, Turkey and northern Iraq. In those countries it is the yellow form which is exotic. The red variety was valued because it bloomed earlier than the English plant, being adapted to the colder conditions of a Turkish winter. It was even called the 'snowy flower' (in Turkish, *Carchichec*) because of its ability to raise its head up above the melting snow. As with the yellow primrose, double forms were produced, but they were not as hardy as the British varieties.

At the height of the primrose craze in Britain during the 1840s many asiatic types were introduced, which were thought to be less difficult to keep, and today there is a large choice of suitable tender types for use indoors.

The most popular of these is the delicate-looking fairy primrose, *Primula malacoides*, from western China. It has thin tall stalks with small fragrant flowers that are white, pink, red, and the original species colour of purple or mauve. Also from China is *Primula obconica*, the poison primrose, which has large flowers clustered on cowslip-like stalks. It gets its common name because the leaves can irritate the skin. Last but not least is the Chinese primrose itself, *Primula sinensis*, found all over China but first collected near rivers in Yunnan province, eastern China, by John Potts in 1821. Hybrids of the Chinese primrose are favoured for their red frilly-edged petals.

One of the most successful indoor hybrids is *Primula kewensis* which looks like an 'artificial' form of the common wild primrose but is a cross between *Primula verticulata* from southern Arabia and *Primula floribunda* from the Himalayas. It is the only yellow-flowering primula especially marketed as a house plant.

There is a wide variety of natural habitats from forests to open alpine, but primulas, being among the first flowers to bloom in the spring, like it cool and moist during the flowering season. Like other spring flowers, by growing before competing plants have had a chance to open up and overshadow them, the primrose can get the best of the spring sunshine and insect pollinators. Similarly, in the house, it likes a sunny spot, but not directly in the scorching sunlight of a south-facing window.

The tender indoor varieties are usually treated as temporary plants though they can be kept for two or three years, being short-lived perennials. After flowering they should be repotted and given cool, airy conditions, with only a little water for their summer resting period. But during flowering in late winter and early spring, they do well from thorough watering and occasional soaking, as well as a high potash fertilizer fornightly feed. Primulas can also be sown from seed in mid-summer.

Radermachera sinica

A popular newcomer introduced to Britain with Thatcherism, possibly because it enjoys dry conditions in our modern homes. In 1993 over a million plants were sold in Europe. *Radermachera sinica* (syn. *Stereospermum suaveolens*), named after J. C. M. Radermacher who was an amateur botanist in Java in the late eighteenth century, comes from south-east Asia (India, China, Java, Taiwan and Indonesia) where it grows as a roadside weed. In the wild

PLANTS *Primula* species
REGION OF ORIGIN China
WILD HABITAT Open forest, river banks
HOME HABITAT Cool rooms such as bedroom; temporary resident
COMMON PROBLEMS Wilting from lack of water and heat

The lady palm comes from the cool, dark highland forests of China and makes an ideal potplant for shady, dry corners.

Radermachera will grow into a small tree which produces yellow trumpet-shaped flowers, though there is no record of it flowering in cultivation. It is related to the trumpet vine and catalpas.

> **PLANTS** *Radermachera sinica* (*Stereospermum suaveolens*)
> **REGION OF ORIGIN** South-east Asia
> **WILD HABITAT** A small tree in sub-tropical forest
> **HOME HABITAT** In a bright location, e.g. entrance hallway
> **COMMON PROBLEMS** Compost needs to be kept always moist otherwise wilting and leaf drop occurs; scorched by direct sunlight

This is a good plant for the modern centrally heated house because it can withstand some dryness, although the compost should be kept moist. It likes a bright location but not full sunlight.

Rhapis excelsa
[Lady palm]

See also PALMS

This comes from high altitude forests of China and grows from 3–3.7 m (10–12 ft) tall as dense shrubby bushes in the wild, but usually only up to 1 m (3 ft) in the home, with fingered, hand-shaped leaves. Some people think it is a very hardy plant but it could be that it is just

PLANTS *Rhapis excelsa*
REGION OF ORIGIN China
WILD HABITAT In high altitude forest
as a bush
HOME HABITAT In any room
COMMON PROBLEMS Scale bugs, which are
white/brown lentil-sized pests; they can be
removed by dabbing with methylated spirit

slow to die! One of its most striking features is
an ability to grow in low light. It can tolerate
almost total darkness, but not indefinitely and
occasionally it must be moved to a lighter spot
to recover. Another useful feature for centrally
heated homes is its ability to cope with low
humidity which affects so many other house
plants. Because it grows at high altitude in the
wild it is used to cool temperatures, and can
even cope with a few degrees of frost. At the
other end of the scale it can survive
temperatures of up to 21 – 26°C (70 – 80°F).

Rhipsalidopsis
See Christmas and Easter cacti

Rhododendron
See *Azalea*

Rosa chinensis minima
See Pot rose

Rosary plant
See *Ceropegia*

Saffron spike
See *Aphelandra*

Saintpaulia ionantha
See African violet

Mother-in-law's tongue comes from arid grasslands,
surviving long droughts by storing water in
underground rhizomes – making it an almost
indestructible house plant!

Sansevieria trifasciata
[Mother-in-law's tongue]

This is one of those magnificent house plants
that are almost indestructible, surviving most
abuse and neglect.

Sansevieria comes from the arid grassland
regions of eastern South Africa. It has a rhizome
which runs just under the surface of the potting
mixture and is very tolerant of a wide range of
growing conditions. The only conditions it
cannot stand are cold and wet. The minimum
temperature for this plant is 10°C (50°F). It can
store water and can survive up to three months
of drought but too much water will kill it.
Sansevierias should not be repotted more than
every two or three years as they have restricted

PLANTS *Sansevieria trifasciata*
REGION OF ORIGIN South Africa
WILD HABITAT Desert scrubland
HOME HABITAT In a warm dry living room
COMMON PROBLEMS Will rot with overwatering and can keel over if repotted too much

growth from poor soils in the wild, which is mimicked in a restricted pot.

Sansevieria was a favourite with the Victorians because it could withstand the toxic fumes from coal fires and gas lamps. It was usually stashed in a corner and then forgotten, but in those days it went under the more polite common name of the 'rattlesnake' plant.

Sarracenia

[Trumpet pitcher]

See also CARNIVOROUS PLANTS

Sarracenias come from the swamps of North America and make very attractive house plants with upside-down umbrella-shaped flowers. They have elegant, tall leaf pitchers which grow up from the ground like elongated ice-cream cornets, topped with a small lid. Insects are enticed to the rim of the pitcher by nectar and the interesting colours, but once they settle on the rim they lose their footing and fall inside. There is even a narcotic in the nectar which helps disorientate the victim and make it stagger around. Once it has slipped inside, the insect inevitably falls into an acid bath of

Sarracenia purpurea

digestive juices at the bottom and there it dies and its remains are absorbed.

Like Venus flytraps, they need a continuous supply of acid or neutral water such as distilled water, and in the summer they enjoy being stood in their pot in a bowl of shallow water. During the spring and summer growing season they also need good light, and of course a ready supply of insects! They flower in April to May.

Because sarracenias are seasonal, their traps grow stunted in autumn and they can be pruned back to short stumps to avoid mould taking hold. Minimum temperature in winter should be 10°C (50°F).

Sarracenias are suffering a twin threat to their wild homes: illegal collecting and drainage of their native boglands. As the southern USA has become more populous, more demand for land has led to the swamps being drained – and without plenty of water the pitcher plants die. Yet the plants are fairly easy to grow from seed and commercially available plants should now be artificially propagated, and not taken from the wild.

PLANTS *Sarracenia*
REGION OF ORIGIN America
WILD HABITAT Boglands
HOME HABITAT Bright windowsills, such as kitchens
COMMON PROBLEM Watering with hard tap-water – they need acid or neutral water

Saxifraga stolonifera

[Mother-of-thousands]

Most saxifrages are mountain plants, growing on sheltered rock screes, cliff edges or rock-faces or on the arctic tundra. So they can tolerate cold windy conditions. *Saxifraga stolonifera* (syn. *Saxifraga sarmentosa*) is a creeping plant of the temperate forests of east Asia – it tolerates cold and is good for unheated rooms, for example conservatories, but it does need plenty of water. It is also good in small hanging baskets, because it trails many slender red runners with small plants at their tips which should be pushed down into compost, but not cut until they have rooted.

Mother-of-thousands was a favourite with the Victorians, probably because it could tolerate cold rooms after the coal fires died out at night. The minimum winter temperature for this plant is 10°C (50°F).

Schefflera actinophylla

> **PLANTS** *Saxifraga stolonifera* (*Saxifraga sarmentosa*)
> **REGION OF ORIGIN** East Asia
> **WILD HABITAT** Temperate mountain forest
> **HOME HABITAT** A cool room but moderately bright, e.g. bedrooms, conservatories
> **COMMON PROBLEMS** Lack of water and heat causes shrivelling; it needs misting occasionally

Schefflera

[Umbrella trees]

The umbrella trees are part of a group of 200 or so evergreen shrubs and trees from tropical and sub-tropical Asia, Australasia and the Pacific islands. Naming of the group is quite confused with the commonly available *Schefflera arboricola* also being sold as *Heptapleurum arboricola*, while *Schefflera actinophylla* is put by botanists into another closely related genus as *Brassaia actinophylla*. Even so, they are all easily

recognizable as tree-like plants with between six to 16 leaflets arranged like umbrella spokes on long leaf stalks.

Brassaia actinophylla comes from Queensland, New Guinea and Java. It grows as a large tree up to 30 m (100 ft) tall, but only up to 2 m (6 ft) in a pot in the home, which is just as well! In the wild, and in greenhouses it has scarlet flowers which hang down from the stem tips in long strands like the tentacles of an octopus, from which it gets its common Australian name of the 'octopus tree'. Unfortunately it very rarely blooms as a house plant.

Schefflera arboricola is a native of the tropical rainforests of Malaysia and other parts of south-east Asia. It grows as a large shrub in the wild, but takes about four years to reach 2 m (6 ft)

PLANTS *Schefflera*
REGION OF ORIGIN South-east Asia,
Australia
WILD HABITAT Tall sub-tropical
rainforest trees
HOME HABITAT In shaded sunlight of large
living rooms
COMMON PROBLEM Wilting from lack of
water, regular misting will help

grown under good conditions in a pot. These
plants are very popular for entrance lobbies to
offices and in large rooms, and currently at
least nine different varieties are sold in large
volume through the Dutch plant markets
at Aalsmeer.

There are tree-like forms, grown around
moss poles, such as *Schefflera arboricola*
'Compacta', bushy forms such as 'Nora', and
also variegated types such as 'Janine'. In fact
they can all be made more bushy by pinching
out the growing tip of the main stem.

Coming from tropical rainforest the
scheffleras require frequent watering, although
in the British winter they slow down and need
less water. The minimum winter temperature
for them is 10°C (50°F).

Selaginella

Selaginellas are close cousins of ferns, and some
species living in deep shade on rainforest floors
have an intense blue iridescence reminiscent of
flashy blue butterflies or beetles. The blue
colour is caused by the cells on the surface of

PLANTS *Selaginella martensii*
REGION OF ORIGIN Central Mexico
WILD HABITAT Damp and warm
mountain forest
HOME HABITAT Shaded terrarium, or kept
humid in bathroom
COMMON PROBLEM Lack of humidity
causes shrivelling

the fronds reflecting blue light and helps them
to filter out the red light needed for
photosynthesis. They are very widespread, but a
commonly kept species, *Selaginella martensii*,
comes from the mountain forests of Mexico. It
grows erect when young, to 15–30 cm (6–12
in), and starts to branch in maturity, producing
roots which trail down in the forest humus for
water and nutrients.

These plants need warmth, plenty of water
and above all high humidity and so make ideal
terrarium plants. They became all the rage in
Victorian times when the Wardian fern case was
invented. The minimum winter temperature is
10°C (50°F).

Sensitive plant

See *Mimosa pudica*

Setcreasea purpurea

This close relative of tradescantia is a native of
north-east Mexico where it spreads over rocky
and stone-strewn areas, rooting down at
convenient spots into pockets of earth. The
stony surface gives some shade to the roots, and
small scrubby bushes give some overhead
protection from the fierce sun. It quickly covers
large patches of ground.

For the house plants too much water gives
sappy, weak, poorly coloured growth. They are
very tolerant of a very wide temperature range,
and grow well in warm rooms which can cool
down to 7°C (45°F) if dry at the root.

PLANTS *Setcreasea purpurea*
REGION OF ORIGIN Mexico
WILD HABITAT Creeping over stony ground
HOME HABITAT Bright light in warm living
rooms
COMMON PROBLEM Yellowing leaves from
underwatering, but allow to dry out between
regular summer watering; reduce watering
in winter

Setcreasea purpurea

Sparmannia africana

These grow as small trees in grassland of eastern South Africa, but confined to a pot *Sparmannia* turns into a small fast-growing bush which demands a lot of water. Its star-shaped white petals and light green leaves make a nice change from the leathery leaves of other tree-like house plants. Flowering takes place in late summer to early winter. The minimum winter temperature for *Sparmannia* is 10°C (50°F).

    Sparmannia has interesting flower movements. When the flowers open they have a spray of stamens shaped like a shaving brush and when these are touched they spray outwards, helping to brush off their pollen on to pollinating insects.

PLANTS *Sparmannia africana*
REGION OF ORIGIN South Africa
WILD HABITAT As trees in grassland
HOME HABITAT Brightly lit spot,
e.g. bay window, but not in direct sun
COMMON PROBLEMS Flowers are not
produced if too shaded in winter, as light is a
cue for flowering

Since they are rapid colonizers in the wild, setcreaseas grow very quickly and need feeding with fertilizers every fortnight during the growing season in spring and summer. They can grow so vigorously that the plants outgrow their pots and become straggly and lose their colour, so they need repotting or cutting back two or three times a growing season. The deep violet purple coloration of the leaves is brought out by intense sunshine, so very bright light is ideal for the best foliage.

    Setcreasea is very brittle, and just knocking into it will break off a long trailing piece, which in its natural environment will fall to the ground and root. Like the other tradescantia types they are sometimes thought of as 'friendship plants' because their cuttings root so easily and can be given to friends as gifts.

Spathiphyllum
[Peace lily]

See also AROIDS

Spathiphyllum comes from the rainforests of northern South America. The original *Spathiphyllum* house plant, *S. wallisii*, comes from Colombia, and there is a larger hybrid of *Spathiphyllum floribunda*, with the Hawaiian name 'Mauna Loa', but again its stock comes from Colombia.

    The Latin name means that the spathe of the flower looks like the leaves. In full bloom in summer it is a beautiful pure dove white, which is one reason for its common name of peace lily. The spathe is green when young, turning white

PLANTS *Spathiphyllum*
REGION OF ORIGIN Northern South America
WILD HABITAT Tropical rainforest
HOME HABITAT Fairly bright bathroom, shady living room with plenty of humidity
COMMON PROBLEM Wilts very easily, so keep moist with good humidity

only when mature, and then curiously it goes green again after blooming.

It needs rainforest conditions to survive as a house plant, being kept warm and constantly moist by misting and a pebble tray beneath its pot. Under these conditions it grows profusely from a creeping rhizomous root, and it can be propagated by splitting its clumps, though making sure that each new clump has a large piece of the root from which to grow.

With its flowers like a small version of the Jack-in-the-pulpit, it too lives in semi shade and its leaves are easily singed by direct sunlight. It makes a good plant for the humid habitat of a bathroom with a window, or if kept humid enough grows well in living rooms. The humidity and plenty of watering is crucial, though, because the delicate large leaves lose a lot of water. But the one saving grace is that the plant can rest during winter in a drier atmosphere so long as it doesn't get too chilly – the temperature must be above 16°C (60°F) – and watering is eased off.

Spider plant
[*Chlorophytum comosum*]

The spider plant, *Chlorophytum comosum*, comes from the semi-arid grasslands of the Transvaal in South Africa, where the rugged environment has helped make it a very tough plant for the home, easy to grow and able to put up with a good deal of neglect. That's probably why it has been grown as a house plant for 200 years and is one of our most

popular pot plants. It is also used to growing seasons with widely fluctuating temperatures: the summers are hot but the winters are cool and there can even be short severe frosts. But be warned if you decide to recreate the winter frosts at home because the leaves will go brown and the plant dies back, so it's best to keep the

Chlorophytum comosum 'Vittatum'

> **PLANTS** *Chlorophytum comosum*
> **REGION OF ORIGIN** South Africa
> **WILD HABITAT** Semi-arid areas
> **HOME HABITAT** Almost any room in the home, or office, in shade or light, making a good trailing plant
> **COMMON PROBLEM** Brown leaf tips from dry soil or cold draughts

spider plant above chilly temperatures, about 7°C (45°F).

Rainfall is not generous in the wild, between about 38 – 120 cm (16 – 50 in) per year, falling mostly in summer, so it can tolerate drought and survive long periods without water. Part of its survival strategy lies in its very fleshy roots, like an asparagus (in fact, it's in the same family) for storing water. This means that the house plant can survive quite severe punishment from being left underwatered. But to keep the house plant lush and healthy, it needs to be kept away from radiators and watered regularly, although the compost can be allowed to dry out a little between waterings. If the plants suffer long drought they can be revived but it takes about a year to fully restore their vigour, so it's a good idea not to let them dry out completely.

They can stand full sun or shade, although good light also helps plants come into flower. They send out long flowering shoots with plantlets throughout the spring and summer. These small plantlets (which do look a bit like spiders) can be easily broken off and repotted into new plants. In the wild the shoots of the Spider plant root down into the soil to form large carpets around the parent plant and colonize the surrounding ground.

Spider plant leaves are usually variegated – they have stripy green and white markings – which come out particularly well in good light. But why do plants like *Chlorophytum* have leaves with green and white markings? It may be camouflage. Leaf miners – those little bugs which leave crazy little brown or white tracks

under the skin of leaves - steer clear of variegated plants, but why they are put off marked leaves is a mystery. Maybe they think another leafminer has got in first; we just don't know.

Spiderwort

See *Tradescantia*

Stag's horn fern

[*Platycerium*]

See also FERNS

There are some 18 species of stag's horn fern from Asia and Queensland, Australia, and all are tropical epiphytes living high in rainforest trees. Their perches often turn dry for short times, so the plants dry out very easily. They adapt to the fluctuations in moisture by developing thick skinned fronds covered with wax. This makes them good at withstanding the dry air of a home, and of course being tropical they appreciate central heating. They also need a weekly soaking in water to keep their soil watered although their compost needs to be well drained and airy to help prevent waterlogging and to imitate the spartan humus of the trees they grow on in the wild. They also

Platycerium bifurcatum

> **PLANTS** *Platycerium*
> **REGION OF ORIGIN** Asia and Australia
> **WILD HABITAT** Growing on trees in
> tropical forests
> **HOME HABITAT** Warm, shady or bright
> positions, good for hanging baskets
> **COMMON PROBLEM** Waterlogging

experience strong dappled light in the wild so as house plants they do well in reasonably well-lit places, although sunshine in Britain is so weak and short during the winter that they suffer. The minimum winter temperature for these plants is 10°C (50°F). Ironically in the summer the light from south-facing windows can be too much for them so they do enjoy some shade from strong sun.

Their other problem when living on trees is a shortage of minerals because there is very little soil to make use of apart from some decaying debris caught in the tree bark or branches. So instead they feed on falling debris such as dead leaves which they collect in large bin-shaped fronds and rot them down into their very own compost heap. They then absorb not only the nutrients from the rotting compost but also soak up the water absorbed there as well. As house plants without their own compost heaps, help is needed to produce minerals by giving a diluted fertilizer during the summer growing season.

The stag's horn ferns are so well adapted to their compost-heap way of life that they even have two entirely different forms of frond: one flat which spreads over the tree's bark like a plate, within which moist debris collects to provide for the plant's root system, and the other shaped like a stag's horn spread outwards, functioning normally for photosynthesis and carrying the spores.

The weight of compost and water in it can become tremendous and stag's horns have been known to grow as large as a small car in the wild, and carry up to 1 tonne in weight before eventually breaking off, often breaking the branch they live on, but it does not grow anywhere near this size as a house plant. They also live for a long time, for 20 to 50 years.

These ferns often have a cosy relationship with ants. The ants live in the bowl of the fronds and bring back rotting organic humus for the fern.

Streptocarpus

Streptocarpus is in the same family as the African violet, and comes from east and south Africa and Madagascar. They are herbs with shallow fibrous roots and they need moisture around their roots during the growing season in summer when they are used to a rainy season. But they need good drainage and their pot soil has to be thoroughly moistened and then allowed to dry out before watering again. Though basically forest dwellers in the wild, they are restricted to banks, stream sides, rock outcrops and tree trunks and need shade during at least part of the day. So wherever they are kept in the home, the plants need shade, moisture and extra humidity.

They frequent rough-grained rocks that weather into a fretted surface rather than smooth-grained rocks with sharp cleavage planes. Sometimes the roots grow in humus or soil that has collected in the rock crevices, sometimes in cushions of moss. No doubt for the same reasons that rough-grained rocks are better than smooth, so they prefer rough-barked trees.

The plants have to endure a dry season usually from about May to September. The leaves may die back but the base of the leaf recovers remarkably fast with the first rain. So

> **PLANTS** *Streptocarpus*
> **REGION OF ORIGIN** Africa
> **WILD HABITAT** Rocky tropical forest floors
> **HOME HABITAT** Warm, humid atmospheres
> **COMMON PROBLEM** Leaf rot from getting
> the leaves wet

during winter allow the house plants to rest by cutting down watering.

They tolerate a wide range of temperatures with a minimum of around 10°C (50°F).

Streptocarpus rexii is the main species that the house plant was bred from, but it was hybridized with many other species of *Streptocarpus*. They have a very quick method of propagation: the leaves can be cut in half, and the cut edge dipped in rooting powder and then pushed a very little way into some compost. New plantlets will soon sprout all along the leaf's edge and can be given pots of their own when they have started to root.

The plants flower during summer and autumn and, of the eighty available types, most have blue or mauve trumpet-shaped flowers with long fleshy leaves.

Some of the species in the wild are surprisingly tough and can survive even when their forest cover has disappeared.

String of hearts

See *Ceropegia*

Sundews

[*Drosera*]

See also CARNIVOROUS PLANTS

Sundews are probably the easiest of all carnivorous plants to grow, and some are so tough they can even tolerate freezing. They belong to the same family as Venus flytrap but use a completely different trap. Their leaves are covered in sticky tentacles which glue down

---

PLANTS *Drosera*
REGIONS OF ORIGIN Almost worldwide distribution, from the Arctic Circle to the tropics
WILD HABITAT Generally from boglands
HOME HABITAT Sunny positions
COMMON PROBLEM They need acid or neutral water, such as distilled water

---

their prey before killing and digesting them.

Most species of sundew are sun-lovers, but they don't like being roasted under the sun and will do well on a windowsill which gets shade part of the day. They also do well in a terrarium and although the plants go dormant in winter they carry on growing well under fluorescent light held 30 cm (12 in) above the plants. Like all carnivorous plants, they need soft or distilled water and should never be left to dry out because their natural habitat is usually in wet bogland. The boggy soil of the sundew's natural home also means that the plants should not be potted in normal compost, or even in live sphagnum moss which they are sometimes sold in (and which can kill them). Instead, the plants can be potted in compost of equal parts sand and moss peat or the peat-substitute coir.

One of the few problems they suffer from is botrytis mould which sometimes kills off the leaves. The disease is caused by too much humidity, often linked with poor light and low temperatures. The dead leaves should be cut off at their base and the plants given a drier environment and more light.

The plants are very easy to grow from seed – in fact, many species seed themselves and become weeds in homes and greenhouses, which might help explain why it is such a successful worldwide genus of plants.

Swift death

See *Chrysalidocarpus*

Swiss cheese plant

[*Monstera deliciosa*]

See also AROIDS

This is one of the world's most popular house plants. The Swiss cheese plant (*Monstera*

The Swiss cheese plant grows in rainforests of Latin America reaching up to 100 ft high searching for light.

deliciosa) is a climbing plant from the jungles of Central and South America, which thrives along jungle rivers and forest openings where there is light and a constant water supply.

The cheese plant's outstanding feature is, of course, its large leaves perforated with holes and slashes. Exactly why it is perforated is a bit of a mystery: one idea is that it helps cool the leaf by fluttering in the air like a fan. Or it might protect the leaves against high winds since monsteras sometimes climb up exposed rocks as well as trees. Another suggestion is that the holes, like the deep-cut lobes of other leaves, let in light to reach leaves below. There might be something in this last explanation, because the more light you grow the house plant in, the more divided its leaves become; if you don't give the plant enough light its leaves remain almost unperforated and the plant's growth will slow down considerably.

While the cheese plant grows in the dark under-storey of the rainforest it has cunning adaptations for catching light. The leaves crane themselves towards the light and the leaf surface has tiny lenses which help focus light down inside the leaf.

Cheese plants are very easy to care for at home. They are exceptionally tough plants and even if the most pathetic specimens are left unloved and unwatered next to scorching hot windows, they still manage to survive. In fact, the usual complaint is that they become too successful – a happy cheese plant will romp away and become too large for its pot and eventually take over a room! And small wonder they grow to great sizes, because even the largest domesticated cheese plants are still only youngsters compared to the wild specimens which reach a height of 20 m (60 ft) or more. Because of its size, it is normal for some of the lower leaves to fall off as the plant matures – don't be alarmed! Given the size, it's a good idea to give Swiss cheese plants a large room like a living room to grow and expand in.

Exactly why the Swiss cheese plant has

PLANTS *Monstera deliciosa*	
REGION OF ORIGIN Latin America	
WILD HABITAT Climbing up trees in rainforests	
HOME HABITAT Large, sunny places such as living rooms and offices	
COMMON PROBLEMS Spindly small leaves in low light; browning edges to leaves in dry air; weeping yellow leaves when overwatered	

become so popular in recent years is a bit baffling, because it was virtually ignored when it was first discovered in Mexico in the early nineteenth century. But some of its success is probably because it is the hardiest of its genus, since it is the only species which grows on rocks or soil as readily as it does up trees.

In the wild, long sausage-shaped aerial roots grow from the stems down to the ground and provide extra anchorage and water and nutrients as the plant climbs up tall trees and rocks. In your living room the aerial roots are not likely to find a nice pocket of compost behind the television set, so they should be tucked into the pot to help the plant feed from its soil. But the roots grow so long and there are so many of them that there is a limit to how many you can fit into one pot, so the best idea is to let most of them dangle outside the pot or cut them off.

The roots actually come in two sorts: short ones which have sticky root hairs and glue the plant to the tree it is climbing on, and the long feeding and anchoring roots.

But in the home, the plants cannot support themselves so they need to be attached to a damp moss-pole, although it is not easy to keep these moist in the house. Regular misting helps.

The cheese plant has large but rather dull blooms which produce edible fruits. Now a word of caution here – most house plants are inedible and in fact some of them are highly poisonous, so the Swiss cheese plant is something of an exception. The fruits look like small upright cylinders, but they are best not

eaten until the seeds inside are ripe because the immature fruits contain sharp crystal-like fragments to deter animals from
eating them.

It should be kept at temperatures of 13 – 18°C (55 – 65°F) in the winter.

Syngonium
[Goosefoot]

See also AROIDS

These are climbers from the tropics of Central America and the West Indies and are closely related to philodendrons, producing a bloom with a yellow spathe and white spadix although they are difficult to flower as house plants.

The stems produce aerial roots which can attach themselves to a moss pole if the moss is kept moist, or they can be tied to a support, or trained up a framework such as room dividers. In the wild the aerial roots help to absorb moisture from the air and tree bark, as well as anchoring the climber to its host.

Because of the humid jungles from which they originally came, syngoniums need to be kept moist, for instance by standing on a pebble tray and with regular misting. They also suffer when the temperature drops in unheated rooms during the winter because they need about 15°C (59°F) throughout the year. They also need to be kept out of bright sunlight because they enjoy the shade.

PLANTS *Syngonium podophyllum*
REGION OF ORIGIN Central America and West Indies
WILD HABITAT Tropical rainforest
HOME HABITAT Moderate shade, humid, warm, e.g. bathroom
COMMON PROBLEMS Death through cold shock from a sudden drop in temperature; problems also with dry air, so use a moist pebble tray or mister or other method of increasing humidity

---

Their leaves are arrow-shaped when young, but all species go through an adolescent goose-shaped phase (hence its common name goosefoot) and when mature the leaves have five to nine lobes or leaflets. *Syngonium podophyllum* with arrow-shaped leaves is now the most popular house plant species.

Syngoniums first appeared as indoor plants on a list of Victorian house plants in 1881, and were introduced only after house plant gardeners felt more confident after keeping the more hardy foliage house plant species such as rubber plants, calatheas, dracaenas and aspidistras.

All syngoniums can be kept bushy by cutting the climbing stems as they form, but *Syngonium podophyllum* 'Emerald Gem' is a naturally compact variety. The plants grow very fast and they often need repotting each year in a rich compost. They also propagate well if you split the clumps on their creeping rhizomes, though make sure that each new clump has a large piece of root from which
to grow.

Tillandsia
[Air plants]

See also BROMELIADS

Without doubt, the most bizarre of all bromeliads are the tillandsias, called air plants. *Tillandsia* has got high living in the air down to such a fine art that it survives in amazing places where no other plant can grow – you often see it in the sub-tropics and tropics of the Americas festooning telephone wires, power cables and anything else it can grab hold of, and some types can hang down in clumps over 8 m (24 ft) long. They have virtually no roots, don't need soil, and can withstand weeks of drought.

Tillandsias are divided into two sorts: the green ones which come from more humid habitats and behave more like the conventional bromeliads, and the grey-leaved types which

can tolerate the driest conditions. These grey tillandsias are by far the weirdest-looking types – they often appear to be dead and come in a range of shapes, like silvery-branched moss or lichen or with corkscrew-shaped leaves. You would hardly know they were alive until they produce small but distinctive flowers.

The secret of *Tillandsia* is its leaves. They are peppered with minute umbrella-shaped hairs which have taken over from the roots as feeding organs by absorbing rain-water, mist or dew. The umbrellas can also move: when they are dry they fold up, but at the first hint of moisture they fold down and absorb the water like blotting paper.

The umbrellas also grow their own sort of miniature gardens. The moist little environment under the umbrellas is a cosy place for very special bacteria, which have the canny knack of plucking nitrogen out of the air and turning it into a plant fertilizer. It's a kind of board-and-lodging arrangement: the bacteria are clothed, fed and watered by the plant's leaf hairs, and in return the plant gets fed one of its most vital nutrients, nitrogen. The fertilizer also supports other useful bugs, such as yeasts and other fungi, which also do their bit towards feeding the plant. So successful is this strategy that some *Tillandsia* species can live in deserts, often perched on cacti.

There are now several species of *Tillandsia* to grow as house plants. You can make air plant 'trees', using bits of dead branches or cork and attaching a collection of tillandsias on to them, by using mastic or sealant glue but without sticking the leaf bases with the glue.

Tillandsia usneoides (Spanish moss) really does look like dry strands of moss or lichen. It grows almost anywhere in the light, and it's easy to hang from bits of bark or virtually any convenient perch and makes a very attractive grey-green piece of hanging foliage.

Front: *Tillandsia stricta*
Back: *Tillandsia usneoides*

PLANTS *Tillandsia*
REGION OF ORIGIN Sub-tropical, tropical Americas
WILD HABITAT Treetops or other solid perches
HOME HABITAT Bright sunny windowsills in living rooms and other warm places
COMMON PROBLEMS Not much goes wrong with tillandsias

The green, bulbous *Tillandsia* (*Tillandsia bulbosa*) is a particularly intriguing plant because it has a special friendship with ants. Its leaves are tightly pressed against the central stalk into a waterproof, empty tank. Ants can wriggle in through the bottom of the tank and take shelter inside the chamber. In return for a home to live in, the ants leave behind their waste droppings and waste food which the plant absorbs through the lining of its tank.

In the mid 1980s when it started to become more fashionable to keep tillandsias over half those sold were probably collected from the wild. They are slow to propagate but in their native countries, such as Guatemala, tillandsias are being reproduced by taking cuttings from a very few wild collected plants kept as stock, and this together with nursery cultivation is reducing the pressure on wild collected plants. Even so it is always worth asking about the origin of the tillandsias you buy.

Tradescantia
[Spiderwort]

This plant grows on the floors and tropical rainforests of Mexico, and South America. It needs constant warmth of 27°C (80°F), high and steady humidity, filtered sunlight, and protection from extremes of climate. There are over 2 m (6 ft) of rainfall at regular intervals throughout the year in its natural habitat.

Good light is needed for strong growth – too

PLANTS *Tradescantia*
REGION OF ORIGIN Mexico, Central and
South America
WILD HABITAT Creeping on moist
forest floor
HOME HABITAT Bright but shaded light
COMMON PROBLEM Too dry in growing
season causes brown tips to the leaves; mist and
water frequently in summer

much light leads to bleaching and scorching of leaves, too little to spindly growth and leaves losing their attractive colourings. They appreciate cool to normal temperatures 13 – 15°C (55 – 59°F) optimum, but will tolerate some cold, down to 10°C (50°F). Very high temperatures such as those in the direct sunlight of a south-facing window will brown the tip of the leaves.

Spiderwort is a light-sensitive plant. It creeps over forest floors, sending down shallow clumps of roots into thin layers of fertile soil from virtually every node – that's why they propagate so easily into plantlets. When they catch more light in small clearings their stems grow less spindly and leaves grow in clumps.

Tradescantia is well known for its variegated white and green markings. But why are plants like *Tradescantia* variegated? There are a lot of theories: to keep the leaf cool, to fake the damage of leafminers and ward off other predator attacks, and to somehow improve photosynthesis. One idea is that stripy leaves like these are typical of woodland plants growing on the forest floor – they are virtually absent in plants growing in open places. The mottling may help camouflage the leaves from leaf-eating animals. Colour-blind animals such as deer find it difficult to see the mottled patterns on woodland floors that are speckled with flecks of sunlight. Because woodland herbs are among the few plants with edible foliage near the ground between late autumn and early spring they are especially vulnerable to being eaten.

Tree ferns
[*Dicksonia* and *Cyathea*]

See also FERNS

Tree ferns are more garden plants than house plants, particularly in the extreme south-west of Scotland and England where conditions are mild enough in the winter to let them survive. But they can be grown indoors as 'babies' for two years before they get too big and have to be grown on in mild wet conditions outside. They don't take severe frost but can be grown in conservatories, and were very popular in Victorian times.

There are two genera, *Dicksonia* and *Cyathea*. *Dicksonia* is the most widely cultivated. It comes from the tropical rainforests, but the hardy ones come from southern New South Wales, Tasmania or New Zealand. They need 'middle-of-the-road' growing conditions and are surprisingly easy to grow – medium light, medium humidity (but never dry), and moist soils. They are not fussy plants though they are somewhat slow-growing indoors.

In conservatories they grow to 3 – 5 m (10 – 15 ft) high in 40 to 50 years, but in the wild they last for 200 years and maybe longer, growing up to 17 m (55 ft) high.

These are ancient ferns which were once part of the temperate rainforests back in the Carboniferous period 240 million years ago, and long before the flowering plants evolved 60 million years ago hence their other name, 'dinosaur ferns'. They evolved to fill the niches that trees fill now.

PLANTS *Dicksonia, Cyathea*
REGION OF ORIGIN Tropics to temperate
Australia and New Zealand
WILD HABITAT Damp forests
HOME HABITAT Large rooms, such as
conservatories
COMMON PROBLEM Lack of water kills
the fronds

Trumpet pitcher

See *Sarracenia*

Tulip

[*Tulipa*]

Wild tulips come from central and west Asia, where they survive the harsh winters and dry summers in mountain areas. The short-stemmed early flowering varieties are used as temporary house plants such as *Tulipa hybrida* 'Apeldoorn'. They need to be kept cool and in bright light.

Tulip flowers are highly sensitive thermometers: open when it is warm and closing when it cools. The movement is made by growth across the flower – fast growth on the underneath of the flower pushes it shut and fast growth on the top pushes it open. In practice, the flowers open during the day and close at night.

One of the odder reactions of tulips was discovered by florists. Cut tulips usually become limp when put in water after cutting, because the water in the stems is at high tension when growing, and cutting creates an air-lock. The flowers normally need a long rest period in water after recutting the stem before they will stand erect again, but if a pin is inserted just below the flower the stem stands up rapidly. It is not clear why this happens.

Bulbs should be buried in soil in autumn and when the shoots sprout in springtime they need to be kept cool – not more than about 12°C (53°F) – in moist soil, mimicking the

---

PLANTS *Tulipa*
REGION OF ORIGIN Turkey, western and central Asia
WILD HABITAT Mountainous, sheltered by rocks or in open grassland
HOME HABITAT Temporary residents during flowering
COMMON PROBLEM Wilting in hot rooms

---

conditions they get in their wild habitat. With the rich stored food reserves in the bulb they don't need artificial feeding.

Tulips were first brought to northern Europe from Turkey through the horticulturalist Carolus Clusius in about 1573. He cultivated several species in his famous gardens at Leiden and from there a craze for growing tulips in Holland began. In the 1630s 'Tulipmania' reached its height with some rare bulbs being sold for more than the price of a house. The wealthy classes went mad and even started paying for tulips which might exist in the future but only existed as richly coloured paintings in paper catalogues. The madness ended in 1638 when an edict was passed to limit the price of bulbs.

Umbrella plant

See *Cyperus*

Umbrella trees

See *Schefflera*

Urn plant

See *Aechmea fasciata*

Venus flytrap

[*Dionaea muscipula*]

See also CARNIVOROUS PLANTS

Few house plants give so much heartache in their cultivation as the Venus flytrap, but take courage because it is not as difficult as it seems.

The flytrap comes from the sandy peat bogs of the Carolinas of America, where it thrives in damp acidic conditions. But despite its name, the flytrap normally catches spiders, earwigs, centipedes and other bugs that creep across the ground. In fact, it goes to a lot of trouble to make sure it catches prey of just the right size – not too large and not too small. The trap is equipped with touch-sensitive hairs which generally ignore small prey but detect larger

Dionaea muscipula

victims. Once the hairs are bent over the trap snaps shut with an ambush that few animals can escape from – it reacts to touch in just one-tenth of a second.

The trap is actually a superb piece of deception. To an insect it looks like a flower which shines bright under the ultraviolet light their eyes are sensitive to, and it also oozes nectar at its edges to tempt the victims into the trap. Once the insect is enticed into the trap the sheer speed of the plant movement ambushes it.

Once the animal is caught it carries on thrashing around inside the trap, and that stimulates the trap's digestive juices to ooze

---

PLANTS *Dionaea muscipula*
REGION OF ORIGIN Carolinas, USA
WILD HABITAT Peaty, sandy bogs
HOME HABITAT Bright, humid windowsills, e.g. kitchen
COMMON PROBLEMS Do not water with hard tap-water – they need acid or neutral water; mould on the traps and leaf stalks – pick off infected material and/or spray with anti-mould chemical

---

from the trap lobes which are tightly pressed together – the vegetable version of a stomach. The creature dies, its remains are broken down and absorbed into the plant for its growth and development.

The problems with growing the Venus flytrap usually come from:

1 giving it alkaline tap-water;
2 too much water which waterlogs it or too little water which dries it out – it just needs a saucer of water under its pot to keep it moist;
3 soil which is too fertile; it needs fairly inert material like moss, clean peat or even vermiculite;
4 poor plants; unfortunately many of the cheaper Venus flytraps are already dying when you buy them because their mossy soil is rotten;
5 mould which the plants are prone to – if traps or their leaf stalks turn black and mouldy cut them off or spray with anti-mould chemicals available from garden shops;
6 feeding it dead meat;
7 overfeeding it – flytraps get indigestion!

Feeding it dead meat or overfeeding it gives the flytrap a very unpleasant version of indigestion which makes the trap rot and smell somewhat. Much better to let the trap catch its own prey – in Britain it is particularly good at catching wasps because of the sweet nectar it secretes at the edge of the trap!

Venus flytraps need to 'sleep' over winter, and one useful tip is to put them in a fridge for several weeks at that time. This gives the plant a hormonal boost which makes it grow even larger the next season.

At the end of the growing season you can easily propagate the plants by repotting them and breaking off their underground daughter corms.

Vriesea

See also BROMELIADS

Vriesea is a very pretty group of striped or spotted bromeliads from the humid forests of

South America, many occurring in southern Brazil. They live near the ground, on rock faces and in the dappled light of the lower branches of trees. The genus was named in honour of the nineteenth-century Dutch botanist, Willem Hendrick Vriese.

Vriesea splendens, the flaming sword, is the most popular species because of its fantastic red flower-spike, which is made from leaf bracts through which tubular yellow flowers peep.

Each rosette of leaves flowers only once before it dies, but new shoots can appear from the base of the leaves or from slightly higher up, away from the potting compost. To root well the offsets should be quite large, about 10 – 15 cm (4 – 6 in) or so, with roots before they are removed. Alternatively the old leaves of the rosette which has flowered can be cut short (they will rot away in time in any case) and the offsets at the leaf base can then be allowed to grow on into small plants before repotting.

Vriesea polemanii

PLANTS *Vriesea*
REGION OF ORIGIN South America
WILD HABITAT Rock faces, lower branches of trees
HOME HABITAT Bathrooms, kitchens with humidity and bright light – but the flowering plant can be placed anywhere
COMMON PROBLEMS Scorched leaves from direct sunlight, dry air

The other advantage of a *Vriesea* plant in flower is that it can be kept pretty well anywhere in the home because it will die anyway. And as the death can take several months – even longer if the plant is kept cool at around 10°C (50°F)– it gives you time to appreciate the plant in all its glory.

Like most bromeliads, however, it does thrive best in a bright warm spot, though not in direct sunlight or the leaves scorch. Moisture from misting and by filling the cup in the centre of the rosette is welcome, occasionally with an added liquid plant food because it feeds through the leaves.

Wax plant
See *Hoya*

Weeping fig
See *Ficus benjamina*

Yucca elephantipes

The yucca is a large tree from Mexico and Guatemala, growing in very harsh terrain with fleshy roots which can search widely for water in deep soil and under rocks. It tolerates a wide range of temperatures and a certain amount of dry air. Water can be stored in the bulky stem and can carry the plant through short periods of drought. The yucca can be grown in south-facing light and sometimes unheated porches. In the summer the plant can even be taken outdoors but it needs to be slowly acclimatized

Yucca elephantipes

PLANTS *Yucca elephantipes*
REGION OF ORIGIN Mexico (Guatamala)
WILD HABITAT As a tree on poor soil
HOME HABITAT Very flexible but need good light
COMMON PROBLEMS Lack of light stops growth; scorching in extremely strong sunlight if placed outdoors suddenly in summer

results. During winter they prefer to be a little cooler if they are not in good light. They can also tolerate hot, dry air, so they are ideal for well-heated homes and offices. Add a little water when it dries out.

The yucca plant is also good at absorbing embarrassing 'pongs' in bathrooms and toilets because its leaves absorb ammonia!

Yucca flowers also have an interesting pollination story. The yuccas' sex lives are tied to certain types of moth. The female yucca moth is attracted to the flower by its nightly smell. The moth climbs up several of the stamens in turn and scrapes their pollen together into a ball. It then transports this pollen lump to another flower, which it carefully inspects to make sure that the stigma is receptive, and that another moth has not forestalled it. If all is in order, the moth lays from one to four eggs in each of the three cells of the ovary and then applies pollen to the stigma.

The ovules into which the moth's eggs have been pushed grow abnormally large and form the food for the emerging moth larvae; but there are plenty left to develop into seeds. As the latter ripen, the moth larvae, now mature, climb down the plants to pupate in the soil.

Not only do the adult moths emerge when the yuccas in their area are in flower, but the pupae spread their emergence over three

since putting it directly into bright sunlight leads to severe scorching.

It needs good light with some direct sunshine each day, but if it is hidden in a dark corner it will not die but simply stop growing. Temperatures as low as 10°C (50°F) give good

The yucca originally came from arid lands of Mexico and Guatamala before it became the trendy house plant of the 1920s; it grows well in sunny places.

seasons, just in case the yuccas have an off-year without bloom. The plant ensures that the moth larvae have food and shelter; the moth guarantees the pollination of the yucca. They are completely mutually dependent. There is, incidentally, a bogus yucca moth, which copies the true species only in laying its eggs in the ovules.

In the wild the stem hardly grows but sprouts a big bunch of leaves. The following year the stem continues its slow growth, but the previous year's leaves die off. This continues for many years and the gigantic crown of leaves rises higher and higher above the ground, reaching up to 14 m (45 ft) tall in often very harsh terrain. For house plants, a yucca can be bought as a stumpy piece of stem, and stood in water to make it root before being potted.

Yuccas are very easy to grow, like dracaenas, and can tolerate temperatures almost down to freezing. If they become too tall they can be regrown from stems. They are pretty indestructible, but do not place too close to radiators, and give them good light and ordinary soil. They get too big for many people, and after cutting they will regrow a shoot from just below the cut.

They are not really native to Guatemala, but have been very widely cultivated there for their white bell-shaped flowers which are eaten by frying in oil with eggs.

Zebra plant
See *Aphelandra*

Zebrina pendula

Zebrinas are related to tradescantias, and grow in Mexico and Guatemala in humid mountain forests. They have two zebra-like silvery green markings on an olive green leaf which is deep purple underneath. Light-sensitive plants, they grow with long trailing stems in shade. Under bright light the leaves become quite small, often

PLANTS *Zebrina pendula*
REGION OF ORIGIN Mexico and Guatemala
WILD HABITAT Creeping plant in undergrowth of humid mountain forest
HOME HABITAT Moderate light away from the window of a living room
COMMON PROBLEMS Loss of colour in poor light; singed leaf tips if kept in a very dry atmosphere.

curled at the edges and with brighter colours, which may be a response to protect themselves from full sunlight.

The zebrina plant is reasonably drought tolerant but brown tips show that the air is extremely dry and the plant should be moved to a more humid room. They appreciate a temperature of about 15°C (60°F). Brown tips can also signify too much light or that it is too cold. It needs medium light, about 1.5 m (5 ft) into a west-facing room. In poor light it loses its purple colour and turns green.

Most tradescantia-like plants including Zebrinas need pruning because they have such vigorous growth. Pruning can be done by pinching out the growing tips, which makes the plant produce more branches and it becomes bushy. Rooted tip cuttings can be potted up to produce new plants. Since zebrinas root so vigorously they can be grown in a very interesting way by placing cuttings in a glass jar or small fish tank filled with water and inert material such as vermiculite.

It is not really known who collected *Zebrina pendula* from the wild in Mexico but it is recorded in Britain before 1850. Sir Joseph Banks, the famous botanical collector, experimented with tradescantia-like house plants which he had obtained in 1794.

Zygocactus
See Christmas and Easter cacti

General Information and Specialist Societies

Please send an sae when requesting information from the following organisations:

BRITISH CACTUS AND
SUCCULENT SOCIETY
49 Chestnut Glen
Hornchurch
Essex
RM12 4HL
Tel: 01708 447778

BRITISH AND EUROPEAN
GERANIUM SOCIETY
56 Shingley Road
Higher Poynton
Cheshire
SK12 1TF
Tel: 0782 783571

BRITISH IRIS SOCIETY
43 Sea Lane
Goring-by-Sea
Worthing
W. Sussex
BN12 4QD

BRITISH IVY SOCIETY
14 Holly Grove
Huyton
Merseyside
L36 4JA

BRITISH ORCHID COUNCIL
52 Weaste Lane
Thelwell
Cheshire
WA4 3JR
Tel: 0925 261791

BRITISH ORCHID GROWERS
ASSOCIATION
McBeans Orchids
Cooksbridge
Lewes
Sussex
BN8 4PR
Tel: 0273 400228

BRITISH PELARGONIUM AND
GERANIUM SOCIETY
134 Montrose Avenue
Welling
Kent
DA16 2QY

BRITISH PTERIDOLOGICAL
(FERN) SOCIETY
16 Kirby Corner Road
Canley
Coventry
CV4 8GD

BOTANICAL SOCIETY OF
THE BRITISH ISLES
c/o Dept of Botany
The Natural History Museum
Cromwell Road
London
SW7 5BD

BULB INFORMATION DESK
Highland Hall
Renwick
Penrith
Cumbria

CARNIVOROUS PLANT
SOCIETY
174 Baldwins Lane
Croxley Green
Herts
WD3 3LQ

CYCLAMEN SOCIETY
Tile Barn House
Standen Street
Iden Green
Benenden
Kent
TN17 4LB

DAFFODIL SOCIETY
32 Montgomery Avenue
Sheffield
S7 1NZ

STREPTOCARPUS
Dibley's Nurseries
Cefn Rhydd
Llanelidan, Ruthin
Clwyd
LL15 2LG
Tel: 0978 790677

EUROPEAN PALM SOCIETY
c/o The Palm Centre
563 Upper Richmond Road West
London
SW14 7ED
Tel: 0181 876 3223
Please send cheque for £1.95 for
catalogue.

THE FAUNA AND FLORA
PRESERVATION SOCIETY
(FFPS)
1 Kensington Gore
London
SE7 2AR
Tel: 0171-823 8899

HYACINTHS
Alan K. Shipp
9 Rosemary Road
Waterbeach
Cambridge
CB5 9NB
Tel: 0223 571064

MAMMILLARIA SOCIETY
Pilbcam
51 Chetsfield Lane
Orpington
Kent
BR5 4HG

NATIONAL BEGONIA SOCIETY
7 Springwood Close
Thurgoland
Sheffield
S30 7AB

NATIONAL CHRYSANTHEMUM
SOCIETY
2 Lucas House
Craven Road
Rugby
Warwickshire
CV21 3HY

PLANT VARIETY RIGHTS
OFFICE
White House Lane
Huntingdon Road
Cambridge
CB3 0LF
Tel: 0223 462727

THE RHS RHODENDRON,
CAMELLIA AND MAGNOLIA
GROUP
Netherton
Buckland
Monacharum
Yelverton
Devon
PL20 7NL

ROSE, CARNATION AND
SWEET PEA SOCIETY,
NORTH OF ENGLAND
94 Hedgehop Road
Westerhope
Newcastle upon Tyne
NE5 4LA

THE ROYAL NATIONAL ROSE
SOCIETY
Chiswell Green
St Albans
Herts
AL2 3NR

SAINTPAULIA AND
HOUSEPLANT SOCIETY
33 Church Road
Newbury Park
Ilford
Essex
IG2 7ET

SCOTTISH ORCHID SOCIETY
Grange View
Lamancha
West Linton
EH46 7BD

SCARLETTS
Nayland Road
West Berg Holt
Colchester
CO6 3DH
Tel: 0206 240466
Supplier of *Phytosalis*

WILD FLOWER SOCIETY
68 Outwoods Road
Loughborough
Leics
LE11 3LY

Index

Page numbers in *italics* refer to illustrations